THE JOYFUL FRUGALISTA

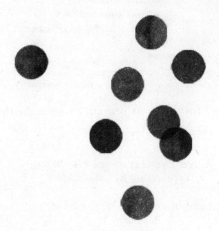

Published in 2019 by Murdoch Books, an imprint of Allen & Unwin

Murdoch Books Australia
83 Alexander Street, Crows Nest NSW 2065
Phone: +61 (0)2 8425 0100
murdochbooks.com.au
info@murdochbooks.com.au

A catalogue record for this
book is available from the
National Library of Australia

A catalogue record for this book is available from the British Library

ISBN 978 1 76052 419 7 Australia

Cover and text design Lisa White
Typesetting by John Canty

Printed and bound in Australia by Griffin Press

10 9 8 7 6 5 4 3 2 1

MIX
Paper from
responsible sources
FSC® C009448

The paper in this book is FSC® certified.
FSC® promotes environmentally responsible,
socially beneficial and economically viable
management of the world's forests.

THE JOYFUL FRUGALISTA

SERINA BIRD

MURDOCH BOOKS

SYDNEY · LONDON

To my Neil, who changed my light bulbs
and stole my heart

CONTENTS

INTRODUCTION

'Wow, you get out a lot,' said a new friend in response to my Facebook and Instagram photos. 'You seem to do some really interesting things.'

Yes, it is true that I get out a lot. I like to dress up to go out to the launch of an exhibition, to the theatre or the opening of a new restaurant. I have too many pictures even for my Instagram account of places I have been and things I have done. But my outwardly flamboyant life is merely a front: I am a frugalista.

'What is a frugalista?' people often ask me. If I said I was a *fashionista*, they would probably understand. A *frugalista* is someone who lives the good life, the fashionable life, while still living frugally — someone who is mindful of the small things, avoids waste and lives consciously. A frugalista prioritises things like reducing food waste and negotiating the best deals, and can identify what is a need rather than a want. A frugalista isn't a slave to department store fashion and instead appreciates what they have and makes the most from it.

As a frugalista, I celebrate the abundance around me, enjoying and knowing that I don't have to be in debt to live my life the way I want to.

I believe in 'less is more' and in striving to live with less clutter, instead focusing on only having those things I use and enjoy. My frugal lifestyle also places a premium on people and experiences over 'stuff'.

WHY BE A FRUGALISTA?

For many years, I kept my frugal lifestyle a deep, dark secret.

Once upon a time, thrift and frugality were celebrated as virtues. Wives were encouraged to be economical in the home and to find creative ways to cook with less and use up leftovers. Cookbooks and magazines were filled with useful tips and tricks for doing more with less.

Yet somewhere, somehow, frugal became a dirty word. I want to reclaim it.

Instead of being equated with negative words such as poor, meagre, paltry, cheap, insufficient or even skimpy, I want frugality to be associated with concepts such as creativity, appreciation, abundance, choice, empowerment and being enterprising and environmentally sound. I don't see frugality as something that imprisons women in the home, forcing them to make do on a meagre allowance, but rather something positive that empowers both women and men.

For many years at work and social functions, I did not talk about my frugal lifestyle. If I was complimented on my dress, earrings or handbag, I would never admit they were from an op shop (or free). I wouldn't share a 'frugal' recipe for homemade items. I quietly brought my own lunchboxes of leftovers to work and eschewed daily takeaway coffees from the cafe.

Then one day a conversation with a life coach encouraged me to be proud of my frugal ways. I felt liberated once I acknowledged to the world that I am a frugalista, especially as I discovered how blessed I was to have many friends who shared similar values.

I am in a good financial situation and don't need to live a frugal lifestyle as such, although that wasn't always the case, as I will explain later. Even though I am now far wealthier than the average Australian, I still need to make choices in order to live within my means. However, I am proud of the choices I make. I am proud that my low-consumer lifestyle is comparatively kind to the environment, and I am proud that by saying no to many consumer goods I am often saying no to products made under poor labour conditions. I love supporting local op shops, church fetes and school fairs. I also find that people give me things they no longer need, as they know I won't be offended by second-hand goods or surplus food. Being a frugalista helps me to attract abundance.

By empowering myself, I am also empowering my children, family and friends, showing them that having your finances in good shape brings security and provides options. I am proud that my savings allow me to invest wisely. My investment properties, for instance, provide shelter for families in need of accommodation.

Funnily enough, I am discovering that a lot of the tenets of my frugalista lifestyle are consistent with modern research about the meaning of true happiness. The Beatles might have sung that 'money can't buy me love', but that's not what advertisers and marketers are telling us. Instead, we are conditioned to think that we need to buy our children's love through toys, computer games and sports equipment. After all, isn't that what we do to bring happiness to our own lives? Rather than confront pain and sadness, we drink a bottle of wine or eat a block of chocolate, or perhaps go out on a shopping binge to help ease the pain through retail therapy. As Brené Brown noted in her powerful TED talk on vulnerability, we don't allow ourselves to be vulnerable, to experience pain as well as happiness.

Well, perhaps I have eaten a bit of chocolate more than once after (or during) a bad day at work, and I don't mind a glass of prosecco for a celebration. I also admit that I dressed myself up in new clothes and make-up after I broke up with my husband—and again when I broke up with my cheating ex-boyfriend. However, I spend within my means, buying cheaply and supporting second-hand charities and even getting things for free. I also avoid going overboard.

My frugalista lifestyle is not one of misery and deprivation. Instead, it is one of fun. Because isn't life about having fun and enjoying the moment? I won't judge you if you want to look and feel good, or if you are being frugal so that you can afford a fabulous holiday. Spending money on things that we enjoy is important. If all you do is work, work and work, then go home and sit in a dark room eating baked beans on toast while dreaming that 'one day' you'll start having fun, you might not recognise what fun is when you get to that day when you allow yourself to be happy.

A FRUGALISTA IS NOT A SCROOGE

One thing that people often say to me when I tell them that I espouse a frugal lifestyle is that they are all for saving money, but they can't abide being with people who are stingy or scroogey.

Being frugal is very different from being cheap. We all know some- one who is cheap—such people are lavish with themselves but stingy with others. If you go to dinner as a group, they haggle over splitting the bill, trying a different formula to maximise their benefit. You see them stealing packets of sugar from cafes or taking too many shampoo and conditioner bottles from hotels. I know people like this, and they are painful to be around.

These people are not frugal: they are cheap and nasty. It is because of people like this—the ones who are scroogey with other people but who are generous with themselves—that the frugalista lifestyle gets a bad rap.

You can still be a generous person even if you don't spend a lot of money. This is because generosity comes from the heart. Consider where the term 'scrooge' came from—Ebenezer Scrooge was a character in

Charles Dickens' novel *A Christmas Carol*. He had a lot of money, but he was mean to his workers and other people he met. He didn't allow love into his life. He wouldn't see family at Christmas. He refused to donate to help those who were doing it tough. I believe Dickens was trying to show that Christmas is a time when we should demonstrate goodwill to others, including those who are in need. Somehow this has morphed into a need to get ourselves into debt to buy presents for people that they don't want or need at Christmas time in order to prove that we are not like Scrooge.

The Australian Securities and Investments Commission's Money-Smart website estimated that the average Australian credit card debt after the 2017 Christmas holiday season would be $1666, and 82 per cent of people would take up to six months to pay off that debt. Three per cent would never be able to pay it off.

Dickens' message was about more than money. It was also about community and relationships—witness Scrooge sitting down eating Christmas lunch with family. I contemplated this issue during a meal with two girlfriends.

'I understand being frugal, but I just can't abide people who are mean,' said my friend.

I agreed with her. Our meal was simple. I made pumpkin soup, which is usually a cheap enough meal in autumn and early winter when pumpkins are plentiful. It was even cheaper for me because the home-grown pumpkin was a gift from a good friend. It was a beautiful deep, dark orange and, because it was grown without pesticides, it tasted truly special.

I served the soup with toasted soy and linseed bread that I got for free; I had helped out with collecting end-of-day bread to distribute as part of my church's food bank program, and there was plenty left over. No, this is not stealing, and involving my kids in the bread collection is a great way for them to learn about generosity towards others.

Because we had things to celebrate, I opened a bottle of ALDI French Champagne to serve with dinner. It wasn't expensive, but it was bubbly and fun. One of my friends brought chocolate to share, and another brought a quiche and some strawberries. It was a simple yet fun pot-luck feast.

I know many people who don't entertain because they worry their house is not good enough, or think they can't host a proper dinner party without serving several courses of expensive food. They go to restaurants instead or, more usually, they just don't share a meal with other people at all.

Last year I went to a dinner party that was like a potluck affair on steroids. The entree was four plates of cheeses, meats, olives and dips. The main was more meat on the barbecue than anyone could finish (especially after the antipasto plate), and the wine just kept coming. My contribution was a simple home-baked limoncello cake, served with homemade limoncello. It was a fun night, but at one point I discovered that the young couple who had brought the entree did not own their own house and despaired that they ever would. Their contribution was delicious and generous, but was it any better than pumpkin soup made with love? Was it worth getting into debt for?

What I am trying to say is that generosity has nothing to do with money. Generosity could be listening to a friend who has just broken up with the love of her life (thanks to all my many friends who nursed me through heartache). Or it might be helping someone proofread a job application, dropping off food to a friend who is sick or has just had a baby, or just asking someone how their day has been (and really listening rather than just talking). Contrast that, for example, with a friend of my mum's, who used to get expensive perfume every year for her birthday. Fine, except for the fact that her husband had no idea what she liked and would send his secretary out to buy it.

As for those people who take things like towels from hotel rooms, this is not being frugal, this is stealing. There is no other word for it. It is taking something that is not yours. It is not okay to take it because you think that the hotel can afford it — it is still stealing.

Why does this matter? Surely no-one notices? Well, in the karma of the universe, you are doing something negative, and there are always repercussions. You are also sending out the message that you need to steal and that you are not worthy of affording things in your right. This is the opposite of generosity and love. People notice, even if you don't think they do, and it does impact adversely on their opinion of you. Is your reputation worth so little that you would throw it away for a couple of hotel towels that you probably don't even need?

LIVING CONSCIOUSLY

There is a name for an aspiration for delayed spending in the personal finance world: Financial Independence, Retire Early (FIRE). The idea is that you work hard and save like crazy so that you can retire at an early age. The media love stories about people who have achieved this. Often these people then seek a second 'job' travelling the world, Instagramming it as they go.

Saving for your future is admirable. Many people are in denial about the fact that you need savings to live on after you retire. Many young people are not contributing as much as they could to superannuation and are thus missing out on tax advantages.

There is, however, one major problem with the FIRE approach: you may die before reaching the 'retire in style' goal, meaning that you have not lived the life that you always wanted to live. If you retired suddenly, would you even know how to start living? Would you, for example, enjoy being around the people you are living with now? Often we are so busy *doing* that we are not living the way we really want to, not appreciating the people in our lives, not spending time with them. I am guilty of not spending time with family and friends, of shunting my kids off to too many activities rather than just being with them, listening to them or sitting down and playing board games with them.

I do not plan to spend years working in a job that I hate so that one day, maybe, I can do something I love. I want each and every day of my life, each and every moment that I live to be meaningful. I want to live consciously. I feel blessed that I have a job that I love, and when I transition out of that, it will be because my energy is being directed to things that are even more significant and meaningful than what I am doing now.

The future does not exist — this is part of the classic mindfulness doctrine. If you think about it, the future literally does not exist. The moment you get to the future it is the present. It's like chasing rainbows — catching the future is impossible. Since all we have is the present, the goal is to manage our money now. Not being able to sleep at night because you are worried about how to pay bills is not a mindful or happy way to manage your finances.

I have strong financial goals, and I am an aggressive saver. I want to be in a situation where, if something happens at work that I morally oppose, if I am experiencing health problems due to stress, or if my children need me to be with them, I have the financial resources to leave my job. I want to know the security of owning my own home, and I pay more than I need to into my mortgage each month. I also make additional contributions to my superannuation because I believe that saving for the future is important. But if I don't spend money on doing things I enjoy or that make my life better, then my money is just a series of numbers on a spreadsheet.

I don't want to be the richest person in the graveyard. I want to live. I want to be able to go, as I did recently, to a wine-tasting event with family and splurge on wood-fired pizzas and gelato. (I had a gift voucher for this, so it actually wasn't that expensive; but I digress.) I want to be able to dine on a five-course dinner with matching wines: I love good food and wine, and I enjoy this. I want to travel to the coast and do tai chi along the beach and have my kids play in the waves. I want to be able to buy concert tickets when a band that I like is touring, to go out and dance, and to drink the occasional cocktail. I love overseas travel and exploring new places, and I have a bucket list of places I want to visit. I also want to explore my own backyard and enjoy memories and experiences here.

The trick is to find a balance between living and saving to invest. The method in *The Richest Man in Babylon*, a classic book of savings stories by George S. Clason, recommends saving ten per cent of your income. You then convert your savings into secure investments, which create an army of golden slaves who work hard to create wealth for you. Wouldn't you rather a golden army of slaves go to work for you every day than commute to and from work, stuck in traffic, being a slave to your boss and your organisation?

How many of us actually save ten per cent of our income? Think back to your first job. Was it in a supermarket? McDonald's? My first job was as a check-out chick at Franklins supermarket. Where is the money you earned now? If you had saved and invested ten per cent of your income from that time onwards and put it in a modest investment such as a high-interest account, how much richer would you be now? Would you have missed that ten per cent of your pay packet? Probably not. But you would most definitely notice the results of your investments now.

In their book *The Millionaire Next Door*, Thomas J. Stanley and William D. Danko outline their results of studying millionaires in the United States. Although published over 20 years ago, this book remains a bestseller because it shows through research that the super-wealthy are super-savers. On average, most mega-millionaires live comfortable yet surprisingly modest lifestyles and save around 20 per cent of their income. They have balance between what they earn and what they spend. They live well, but within their means, they are interested in amassing real worth rather than buying trinkets to impress others, and they are inconspicuous in their spending and lifestyle.

All of this resonates with me, because previously, in the pursuit of FIRE, I was missing out. My ex-husband and I amassed ten properties together in less than ten years. Neither of us had a large income, and in fact, I earnt considerably more than him. For around ten years we scrimped and saved. We had homestay students and we prepared three meals a day for them. We rarely went out. Although we had a few good trips together, we rarely travelled and we certainly travelled much less than our friends.

Life wasn't miserable, but I couldn't do many things that I wanted to as money was always tight. We were overcommitted financially, and we lived from payday to payday to ensure that we could make payments on the mortgages. I found living with this debt burden stressful. I felt that it locked me into the same job and the same way of life. There was no flexibility. And it seemed that the moment we got ahead, we would just go out and buy another investment property and be in debt again. Or something in one of the investment properties would go wrong, and we would need to invest in major repairs.

One day I asked the question of my (then) husband: 'Why are we doing this?' In his culture, you worked hard and saved hard so that you could build an empire for your children. He didn't understand where I was coming from and thought we were on the same page. He didn't know where to begin to explain the importance of long-term investing. I didn't know how to explain to him that I didn't want to wait until I was a grandma in a wheelchair to make that trip to Positano that I had always dreamed about. What was I working so hard for if it was not to enjoy the life that I had always dreamed of? What was the point of having a lot of money if I couldn't sleep at night because I was worried about not having enough money to make my mortgage payments?

MONEY CAN'T BUY LOVE, BUT IT DOES BUY POWER AND CHOICES

Ultimately, the frugalista lifestyle is deeper and more fulfilling than just what you look like on the outside. Being a frugalista is about financial empowerment. In our modern society money is a medium of exchange, but it is also power, whether we like it or not. My dad pointed out that, more than power, money is security. We tend to worry more about money when we don't have it. We also tend to worry about money when we have relationship problems because we don't feel secure.

That said, money is functionally important to living a good life. While some doctors and clinics bulk bill, in general having money gives us access to better healthcare. Money can pay for optimal education, for us and for our children. Money gives us choices about where to live and enables us to follow our dreams. Whether it is saving for a deposit for a home of your own, studying at Harvard, walking the Amalfi Coast, skiing in Canada or having the courage to quit your job to develop that crazy business idea that has always been in the back of your mind, having money helps make things possible. And yet we have so much guilt and misunderstanding about money.

Jesus said that it was harder for a rich man to pass through the eye of a needle than to go to heaven. He said this after he offered a young man the opportunity to join his group, to travel with him and explore his spirituality. Imagine that: a spiritual mentor with thousands of fans comes to town and offers you the opportunity to join his elite group! Imagine being offered to join the team to learn from someone even more inspiring than modern-day gurus such as Oprah Winfrey, Richard Branson or Deepak Chopra.

But the man turned down the opportunity because he was worried about leaving his business and investments. In short, he did not seize the opportunity because his money was a noose around his neck. Instead of holding you back from the spiritual experience or trip of a lifetime, money can enable you to go and do what you want with confidence. You can control money; it doesn't control you.

No matter what some detractors might say, the Bible is not against investing in money. Jesus delivered a parable about stewardship, about how three servants were given money and told to invest. One hid the money underground to avoid it being stolen and was scolded for not investing the money wisely. Are you hiding your money underground out of fear? Are you missing a golden opportunity?

When you don't respect money, it leaks out and slips through your fingers, disappearing never to return. When you have a handle on your finances, you have the resources and confidence to do amazing things with your life. It's strange, but somehow knowing that you have financial reserves means that you can be prepared to take risks and try new things.

Do you dream of winning the lottery and becoming an instant millionaire? Do you believe that you will find happiness when your numbers finally come up and you make it big?

My step-grandmother once painted a picture of her husband sitting in his armchair with a glass of beer in his hand. The work is titled 'Despair'. In the painting it is Saturday night and he is miserable. His numbers didn't come up on Tattslotto (again), and neither did he have a win on the TAB. He is waiting for something to change for his life to start. This painting mirrors his real-life existence. Sadly, he died without winning Tattslotto. (Actually, he choked to death on lobster while on a holiday in Fiji, on a trip paid for by his son-in-law. Perhaps his numbers did come up, in a way.) His life, as I remember it, mirrored that painting. He kept waiting for that moment when he would finally be happy, when he would finally strike it big, yet that moment never arrived. Do you want to spend your life waiting?

THE FUTURE OF WORK

There has been a lot of negative media about rising house prices in Australia, and the difficulty that the Y and Z generations are facing in their quest to buy a house. Demographer Bernard Salt's quip that young people could afford to buy a house if only they gave up eating avocado smash brunches led to an angry backlash from young Australians.

I have several friends and colleagues who fit into this age bracket and I understand their frustration. Wages have stagnated in recent years and they are not keeping pace with the cost of housing. But what really concerns me is that many people have given up on the quest to save any money at all. They just don't see the point.

A young guy at work, a few years into his career, told me that he had done the avo smash sums and giving up his lifestyle was not worth it. He said he could only save around $100 a week, or $5000 a year. Given the rate at which housing was rising, this priced him out of the market so he figured there was no point in even bothering. A young man, in a stable professional job, not yet married or with children, with no savings.

If you took $100 and invested it every week, at the end of the year, you would have not just $5200—given the miracle of compound interest, you could have much more. Superannuation savings would also have tax advantages. If you invest wisely, you will multiply your savings. Whether or not home ownership is a goal, saving is important to ensure there are funds to cope with contingency—because you never know what life will throw at you. And the future of work is poised to be especially disruptive.

In 2016 I was chosen, along with 35 other Commonwealth public servants, to participate in a pilot 12-week innovation course run by the Australian Futures Project. We worked together to find a solution to one of the key Industry 4.0 problems: the future of work.

A large part of our challenge involved understanding what the future of work is. No-one knows exactly what the future holds, but everyone who has thought about it realises that it is going to bring massive disruption, along with many opportunities. Computers changed the workforce, making typing pools unnecessary. The internet era changed the way we communicate globally. But the future of work is going to shake things up because our notion of having a professional job for life will, for many people, be gone forever.

In the future, a university graduate will not necessarily get a stable, full-time contract. This trend has already started. An enterprising graduate will, however, have many opportunities for interesting flexible work such as in the 'gig' economy — if she or he is agile and enterprising. This increased flexibility will enable many people to manage their work/life balance better, to work on their terms, when and how they feel like it. It will even foster innovation and creativity.

It does, however, mean that the traditional 'work until you retire on your superannuation' model is, for many people, no more. With uneven income streams, saving and investing a portion of your income will become even more important. This is not just for retirement, but to cover unexpected and everyday living expenses.

Owning a home will, for many people, also become more difficult. Even with a good savings record, it will become more difficult to convince banks and traditional lenders that you can repay a loan if you do not have a permanent, full-time job. Robust savings and investing will thus become even more important.

I don't feel pessimistic about the future of work. In our case, the team pitch about adopting a communications strategy to build awareness of the future of work (The Future of Work is Here) was adopted by the Australian Public Service Commission. This demonstrated to me that we understood the need to think and do things differently. I think there will be tremendous opportunities for the future of work, and I look forward to embracing them. But it is not enough just to adopt future work; a future savings and investing mindset is also required.

CHAPTER 1

LIVING LARGE

Choosing an abundance mindset

FROM FRUGAL BEGINNINGS

I am not your average middle-aged woman. I am a single mother of two young boys, newly remarried. I am a domestic violence survivor. I am a career woman, award-winning writer, blogger, food reviewer, fluent Chinese linguist and lover of life. And I am a millionaire, with a net worth of around $1,000,000 including investment properties and hoping to double my net worth by 2020.

I have always been a frugalista in some way, shape or form. My dad says that I come from a long line of frugal ancestors. I was raised with strong principles of thriftiness and frugality, and also of the importance of community service. But if you met me at work or while out at a restaurant launch, you would never pick that I was a frugalista unless I raised it as a topic.

My mother, Lee Bird, is a fashion designer. Now retired, she was for many years an icon in the Queensland fashion design scene. I grew up in Noosa Heads, where she had a boutique on Hastings Street. She was, and still is, the epitome of style, and we always lived in nice houses. Growing up, I was often unfairly branded as a spoilt rich kid. I learnt early on not to give out my address except to close friends. I learnt that people have biased views about money. Often people had decided to hate rich people, or that other people's riches had been obtained by ill-gotten means.

But behind the stylish clothes and homes was a different story. My mother had grown up in a poor, working-class household. The family home in Preston, Melbourne, didn't even have a backyard as such—their garden was a concrete slab with a Hills Hoist clothesline in the middle. As a child, my mother dreamed of one day owning a home with a swimming pool.

By the time I was born, my mother had a successful fashion design business and my dad was comfortable as a Commonwealth public servant. We moved to the fashionable seaside suburb of Brighton in Victoria when I was a toddler. I could easily be mistaken for someone who grew up with a silver spoon, who could have whatever she wanted. Except that my mother was determined not to raise spoilt children with a sense of entitlement.

If I wanted pocket money, I had to earn it. From around the age of ten, I spent many school holidays labouring with the seamstresses and junior helpers in Mum's factory, learning to unpick garments, sew on buttons and cut out applique shapes. I was quite good, if I do say so myself, at crocheting and knitting shapes, and doing fringing. Some weekends I would help at fabric sales, where Mum would sell off odds and ends for profit.

I remember even at a very young age that I wanted to be wealthy. I wanted to be fabulously rich, and I understood early on that the way to achieve this was to work for a living rather than to inherit wealth. I never had any expectation that I would be assisted to get where I wanted to be. I was proud to pay my own way with most things, and I was very independent — my mum never gave me handouts, and I was encouraged to be my own woman.

My first real job was as a check-out chick at Franklins, a low-cost supermarket that rivalled Woolworths. I attended a private school that churned out socialites who were expected to marry well. But being short, chubby, academic and on the school debating team, I had no such ambitions. Instead, I noticed two things. Firstly, that you could spend a lot less feeding and looking after your family if you bought at low-cost supermarkets and bought items that were on special. And secondly, how many wealthy people who lived in my suburb shopped at discount supermarkets.

Later, I went on to work at a Harris Farm Markets outlet. Stuffing bags of carrots did nothing for my fingernails, but it did help me develop a strong understanding of the importance of buying and eating according to the seasons. I noticed what time of year fruit and vegetables were at their best and noticed how they were radically cheaper when in season. These were skills I would later utilise in crafting meals that cost $5 or less to make.

Meanwhile, at home, my sister and I learnt many frugal lessons from our stylish mum. Outwardly she looked the affluent part of a successful fashion designer, which she was. But at home, we lived and ate simply, rarely dining out but always eating well. On Saturdays, my sister, Mum and I went shopping together. We usually avoided the major shopping centres in favour of cheaper, local stores. After we came home, we would all cook together to prepare meals for the week. My mum laughs about how this 'batch cooking' technique has become trendy now.

My mum wasn't my only frugal influence. When I was little, my sister and I spent many holidays growing up with my nana, Irene Barron, and my grandfather, 'Woka' Kelvin Barron. They lived on a farm near Whittlesea, and then later moved up to the Sunshine Coast near where we lived.

I was close to my grandmother. She would spend hours curling our hair into Shirley Temple-style ringlets (with cloth, as this was cheaper than hot rollers). She taught my sister and me to knit, to crochet, to tat and even to spin wool. We played card games (she was a ruthless opponent). We spent many childhood hours doing things that my kids would think were boring. We didn't have computer games then, and other than watching *Romper Room* or *Playschool*, doing craft and cooking, there wasn't much to do.

I adored Nana and loved spending time with her. She had been a talented artist in her youth, working at a company that made neon signs. When she was 16, the company was commissioned to make a neon sign for the Skipping Vinegar company. As the youngest person there, she was asked to skip for hours so that they could use her movements as the model for the sign. Thus she became the muse for a modern Melbourne signpost, the Skipping Vinegar sign, aka Audrey. Not that you would know she was famous to meet her. She was incredibly humble and down to earth. And she was very frugal. She would get angry if we used a tissue only once before throwing it in a bin. She preferred handkerchiefs and always had a range of neatly pressed ones handy (more often than not she had crocheted the edges herself as well). Her kitchen was full of bits of plastic wrap, which she reused two or even three times (I have inherited this habit from her). The teapot was always emptied into the garden to help fertilise the lemon tree.

Nana was also a good cook, especially when it came to sweets. My sister has Nana's cookbook, with yellowed recipes written in her flourishing scrawl and her favourites marked as 'extra special'. Nana loved to host morning tea for the neighbours. Her table would groan under the weight of Hello Dolly slice, lemon lattice biscuits, fairy cakes (not the modern larger and fancier cupcakes), liquorice allsorts slice, cheese biscuits, scones and sandwiches. She would lay the table with a lace tablecloth and bring out the Royal Albert teacups and crystal glasses.

Her guests felt like royalty. My special ritual was choosing which teacup set: would I go for pink roses or blue forget-me-nots?

Nana is now in an aged care facility, so most of her possessions have been given away. My sister, my cousin and I inherited the china teacups and crockery. The Royal Albert had been a gift from Nana's sister, Auntie May; the two sisters would gift teacups to each other. My sister and I liked this tradition so much that we now gift teacups to each other. They are relatively cheap to pick up at op shops and church fetes, and we are always on the lookout for interesting designs.

SUDDENLY SINGLE

On the outside, I had a perfect marriage. While on a posting to Taiwan, my ex-husband and I regularly attended cocktail functions, banquets and gala balls. People often complimented us on how good we looked together. But the situation at home was a different story. It wasn't something I talked about. I was overseas and alone.

In August 2014, six months after returning from Taiwan, I went to the Australian Capital Territory Magistrates Court and was successfully granted an interim Domestic Violence Order. I obtained another order in August 2015.

Domestic violence is complicated, and every situation is different. In my case, my ex-husband is a doting father to our children and we have a co-parenting plan in place. As his wife, I loved him. I wanted to nurture him, to stand by his side and help him. But eventually, I recognised that I needed to break the cycle. I needed to get out and I needed to take my boys with me. Nothing would have changed if I had stayed. It perhaps sounds strange, but my decision was one of love, based on self-respect. I decided that I was worth more.

The first six months were the hardest. I was fortunate in that my children and I had a roof over our heads. The Magistrate had ordered me what is known colloquially as a 'kick out order': that is, I was able to remain in the family home and my ex-husband was ordered not to approach the kids or me. It was sudden, and at the time I worried that it was too harsh a measure. Yet I am here today and able to write what I am now writing. Would that have been the case if I had stayed? Or if I had tried to leave without the protection of a court order?

My dad came to stay with me for a while during this process. He had seen enough to understand that I needed support. He was a rock, and he helped with some of the initial legal bills. Still, it was a struggle—a huge struggle—to pay for the mortgage (and the other mortgages), child care, legal bills, groceries and all the expenses that come with raising kids. At times it seemed insurmountable. At times I wondered if I would make it through, if I would end up bankrupt and destitute, or whether I would lose my career and everything I had spent so long studying and working for.

My mantra was, and still is, 'one day at a time, one thing at a time'. I had long believed in the benefits of mindfulness, but I wasn't consciously channelling it at the time; I was just coping as best as I could. I was, however, conscious that if I didn't have the stability of my public service job, if I couldn't earn an income, then I would not have been able to leave.

Having gone through it myself, I am a strong advocate for supporting working women who are experiencing domestic violence. The issue is bigger than just domestic violence leave. A woman needs to feel safe at work, and especially she needs to feel safe when travelling to and from work. She is especially vulnerable when walking to a car or bus stop at night. She also needs to be able to pay for expensive legal fees, counselling and, in many cases, to physically move houses. In my case, being able to hold down a job was vitally important for rebuilding my shattered self-esteem. It also gave me a strong sense of security. I don't know if I would have had the courage I needed if I had not had a permanent job.

Throughout it all, I wondered how an outwardly successful woman who had attended a private school and had four degrees, and who was in fact the main income earner in her marriage, could have ended up as a domestic violence victim. Violence had not been part of my upbringing. At least, so I thought at first. Then I remembered stories my mother had alluded to about growing up. About my grandfather coming home drunk after the six o'clock swill. About my beloved nana, my mum and aunts hiding in the one room with a bolt on the door and trying to stop him coming in. About my mum begging my nana to leave, and hearing the response, 'But where would we go?'

There is now a lot more awareness about domestic violence in Australia and support for victims. However, there was limited support and understanding when I lived in Taiwan—for starters, women often lose access to their children if they divorce. Still, there is a stereotypical view in Australia that the only 'victims' are uneducated, unintelligent, submissive women from lower socioeconomic backgrounds, and that many are Indigenous women. The reality is different. As I have shared my own story, others have shared with me what they have experienced. Beautiful, kind, successful, articulate women (and men) who hide within themselves the pain of their upbringing or relationships that went sour. It can and does happen to women (and men) anywhere.

It is easy to blame the men, but while statistics indicate that 85 per cent of domestic and family violence victims are women, I acknowledge that men can also be subjected to abuse in relationships. Emotional or physical violence towards anyone is inexcusable. I am a pragmatist: I believe it is vital for women to have the financial means to get out. I know that I would not have been able to leave my marriage otherwise. Yes, it was an expensive exercise, and my financial worth took a huge beating. Freedom, however, has no price tag.

ALL THAT GLITTERS IS NOT GOLD

Overall, I have very little debt, and I certainly do not have much consumer debt. I don't own a car (I gave my car to my dad and we now use my husband's car). I don't have a credit card—I use a debit card for online purchases. I own two small investment properties in my own name, and two more with my husband. My mortgage is around $100,000 (and decreasing rapidly).

Many of my colleagues earn more than me. They live in bigger houses than mine. They have big TVs and surround sound systems and all the various mod-cons that go with it. They go on regular overseas holidays. They buy the latest fashions. They buy at least one coffee at the office cafe every day and buy their lunch there as well.

However, I know from talking with these colleagues at social events that they are not always tracking as well as I am. Some cannot afford to buy a house of their own or, if they can, they are facing the prospect of a large mortgage that they don't expect to pay off in their lifetime. Some friends don't like their jobs but feel trapped because they need to buy things for their kids. Raising children is expensive. Often the financial concerns spill over into relationship problems, because it's hard to be chipper and pleasant if you are constantly worried about how to pay the bills—or worse, if you are so stressed about money that you can't sleep at night.

Years ago, while at university, my ex-husband had a part-time job working for a major bank. Every morning he would start at 7 am, opening letters containing cheques for credit card payments. Sometimes he would see details of people he knew. Outwardly they seemed to be doing well because they had a big new shiny car and lived a flashy lifestyle, but he could see from the paperwork that they were in serious debt. One day he had an epiphany that what you see on the outside doesn't always reflect the reality of a person's financial situation. A person might *look* successful and wealthy because they have a new car and a big house, but that doesn't mean they have the money to pay for it. More recently, on the dating scene, I found out about this the hard way through a relationship with a flashy man who was in debt (I nicknamed him Mr Red Sports Car).

In Taiwan, especially when I lived in the south, I often found real wealth when I least expected it. The owner of the Chinese language school where I taught looked and acted like the janitor. My homestay family owned a successful plastic manufacturing factory, yet my homestay father wore cheap polyester shirts. People who ran small street food businesses sometimes had such incredible turnover that they could buy properties in cash.

Reading stories of billionaires, I also began to realise that many of them were exceedingly frugal. Investor Warren Buffett, Facebook creator Mark Zuckerberg, Mexican magnate Carlos Slim Helú, IKEA founder Ingvar Kamprad and Wal-Mart legend Sam Walton could afford to eat caviar every day, yet instead make (or made) day-to-day choices that are probably more frugal than those of most people.

What this shows me is that all that glitters is not gold. True wealth is often not where you think it is. Trying to keep up with the Joneses or leading a Fear of Missing Out (FOMO) existence that you can't afford will only put you in debt.

There is a better way. And that way is to take control of your finances, to learn to live within your means, to aim to create more wealth and to develop a savings plan.

Of course, that doesn't mean life has to be boring. Being a frugalista can be fun and stylish, and lead to real savings and spending habit changes. It's helped me to lead the life I've always dreamed of—I truly am a joyful frugalista.

THE ABUNDANCE MINDSET

There are a number of writers and bloggers who focus on savings and personal finance. Most preach the virtues of living simply and not spending. Consumerism is evil. Many of these sources have been hugely inspirational for the decisions I have made to live the life I lead and I have picked up numerous tips from them. It was revolutionary to realise there were other frugalistas out there.

However, I have found that often these websites, groups or books preached an idealistic and perfect view of frugality. Spending any money was bad. The focus was not on wealth creation at all, but rather on how little money there was and how desperately people needed to 'save'. If you always focus on debt, that is what you manifest in your life.

The underlying themes in my philosophy are self-worth, abundance and gratitude. It's not about racing to have a certain net worth by a certain date in competition with others. Rather, it's about balancing appreciation for what I have with creating the future that I want to live. It is less about 'having it all' and more about thinking mindfully about what I have, and what I want to have. It is about recognising the abundance around me and feeling empowered to make the right choices with money.

I am a big advocate of the law of attraction. I believe that goal setting and visualising are important for achieving the almost impossible, and I have many examples in my life that prove this. For example, I was told that I could never have children other than through IVF, yet I conceived two healthy children naturally.

I have decided that I will be a billionaire. Yes, this sounds crazy, but I have faith that I will get there, dollar by dollar. There is power in expressing gratitude for the fact that what you want is manifesting. I am extremely grateful for the abundance that is already in my life.

I have realised that the fabulously wealthy respect money. They understand how money works. They are not scared to aim high in the achievement of wealth. They are not scared to visualise dizzying abundance. But they respect that abundance and do not fritter it away on trashy things that do not add value to their lives. Instead, they focus on their goal of generating even more abundance.

Often, we hold ourselves back because we have a negative conversation with ourselves about money. We think that we don't deserve money, or that we are not good enough to earn a good wage. Maybe we have a chance to apply for a promotion, but we talk ourselves out of it because we couldn't work the extra hours, or don't want the responsibility. Instead, we think that rich people are greedy, manipulative, dishonest and unspiritual, and justify our acceptance of lack.

I have done a lot of work over the years to change my conversation about money. Yes, I am frugal, and I do things like live on a grocery budget of only $50 per week and forage for edible weeds and herbs. But as I do these things I contemplate my blessings, the fact that I am so lucky to live in this amazing country, to live in my convenient city apartment and to have abundant meals on my table for my family.

I still sometimes find myself having limiting beliefs about money. For example, I once thought that I would be unable to hold down a well-paid executive job because as a single mother of two young children I was unable to work long hours. Likewise, I had told myself that I couldn't get promoted because there was too much competition, and as a single mother I would be seen to be on the 'mummy track'. Every time I identify a negative thought like this, I realise that it is a limiting belief and instead find a new positive affirmation to replace it. It can take time to overcome a limiting belief, but the results are worth it.

What is your conversation about money? Did you grow up thinking that rich people are bad? Or that you aren't smart enough to be rich? Or that working to earn money is a struggle? Did you grow up in a household where there wasn't enough food? Or were you given whatever you wanted without having to work much for it?

If you find yourself thinking negatively about money, imagine instead being surrounded by golden coins. Shake up coins in a glass jar and hear them tinkle. Pin up a $100 note (real or a picture) to your wall and contemplate it. Write yourself a cheque for the amount that you would like the universe to give you. Or try this cute little ditty, which I picked up years ago from the Simple Savings website and have used when times are down:

I'm a money magnet, money comes to me—
More cash money than you ever did see.

FRUGALISTA CHALLENGE

What are your values about money? Do you have any limiting beliefs that say that you are not worth much, or that having money is somehow bad? Write down any negative thoughts about money, then rip the paper into tiny pieces and throw it in the garbage. Those negative thoughts are gone forever. Now write something positive about the abundance around you, using the lined pages at the back of this book. How much money do you want in your life? Write it down and feel that you have that money in your life.

CHAPTER 2

GET SMART ABOUT SAVING

Why every dollar counts

ONE DAY AT A TIME

'Every dollar counts' was my mindset in those dark days when I was newly separated. I was fortunate, compared with many other women who separate with young children, in that I had a secure public service job. But I had a lot of debts in the form of investment property mortgages, and also a lot of expenses (principally mortgage repayments, childcare fees and legal fees).

In the first few months, my focus was on making it through each day. I tried not to worry about the future. It was too easy to get caught up in 'what if' scenarios around not being able to pay bills on time, or think about what would happen if legal processes became drawn out or even if I got sick and couldn't work. I just focused on my mantra: 'one day at a time, one thing at a time'. By tackling each task as it came up and then moving to the next, I was able to rebuild and get on with my life quickly, although it didn't feel quick at the time.

I took a similar approach with my 'every dollar counts' mindset.

My objective was to rebuild, one dollar at a time. It felt daunting, but by concentrating on the small things over which I had control, I convinced myself that I was demonstrating the habits that would ensure prosperity in the long run.

My immediate concern in those days was paying my bills while still building my savings and avoiding amassing credit card or other debts. Because my ex and I did not yet have property-related consent orders in place, most financial issues were joint commitments. I wanted to save money, but it was difficult to do it via my preferred method of paying down my mortgage, as that was still in joint names. Instead, I used to withdraw an amount of cash from my salary each fortnight. The amount varied, but at first it was $450. I used this money for groceries, petrol, doctors' visits and treats at the cafe at work. If I had any leftover money, I put it aside as savings towards Christmas.

Even when I didn't have much money and was worried about debts, I understood the importance of savings. A lot has been written about the psychology of money and investing. Having your own savings, your own money, and watching it grow is powerful. As my savings grew, I found myself believing that anything was possible. Maybe it was only a few coins left over at the end of the fortnight, ten or twenty dollars saved here and there, but it was significant. It was powerful. It stated my intention to save money and accumulate wealth.

I have noticed a tendency for people to complain that 'if only' they earned more money, or 'if only' they didn't have urgent car repair issues, or 'if only' they didn't have to pay such high rent or child-care fees, then they could finally begin to save. And then also there is the attitude that such and such costs 'only a few dollars' so it doesn't really matter in the scheme of things. I often heard people say this when I lived in Taiwan—the Australian dollar was high at the time and local living was cheap compared with Australia. It cost less than 50 cents to buy a coffee at the 7-Eleven downstairs from my office, and only a few dollars to buy freshly baked bagels for breakfast. A five-course meal at a five-star hotel cost around AUD$33 (those were the days!). But my attitude has been, and always will be, that every dollar counts. Every single dollar.

THE POWER OF LITTLE SAVINGS

I had an interesting discussion with my good friend and blogger Evangeline from Nilbarcodefood about the power of little savings. She said that it was paramount to get the structural things right, and then the little things don't matter so much. In her case, she and her husband paid off the mortgage on their unit, so lived rent and mortgage free before upgrading (with a small mortgage) to a house with a garden. They also cycle a lot rather than drive (or used to before babies!), and Evangeline cooks some amazing meals from scratch. These major savings enable them to do other things like save, invest and go on holidays.

Outwardly, neither Evangeline nor her husband present as poor. They live a normal middle-class life, yet have obtained a degree of financial independence that many people can only dream of—at a young age. Their mortgage-free apartment was even featured in a glossy lifestyle magazine. I have friends with style!

I agree that it is important to get the big decisions right. I have seen so many people make stupid, careless decisions with their money. Buying a McMansion that is too big or in the wrong area is one, and making poor decisions about vehicles is another. In my own extended family, I have seen people overcommit to high-priced car loans and how difficult it then becomes for them to focus on saving for a home of their own. However, I also think that the little things, the little savings wins, matter for several reasons:

1. Most wealth creation is done steadily over a long period of time.
   It is a cumulation of focus and effort, and it is the cumulative effect of

the trickles and droplets becoming a ripple, then a stream and then an ocean. As the saying goes, watch the pennies and the pounds will look after themselves.

2. **Saving money is about good habits.** If you don't develop good savings habits now, even if you suddenly become a millionaire you won't be able to save money. Ever wondered why people who win millions in lotteries don't tend to hold on to the money? There are a lot of complex reasons for this, but one of the major ones is that they never had a savings or investing mindset to begin with. If all you do is spend, then that's what you will always do, no matter how much money comes into your life. The more you earn, the more you will spend.

3. **Saving is about discipline.** Years ago, my former mother-in-law was given a cute money box in the shape of a little monk by the nuns at her Buddhist temple. She was instructed to put $1 or, even better, $2 in the money box and to return the full box to the temple at the end of the month. The exercise was a fundraiser, but more than that, it was designed to demonstrate mindfulness. This is because there is power in regular and concerted saving. Just like physical exercise, it is important to practise saving money every single day as it helps to train your mind about the value and importance of saving money.

4. **Little money habits are often habits you repeat tens of hundreds of thousands of times.** It could be that expensive coffee you buy at a cafe every day (even though you could make one at the pod machine at work). Maybe it's withdrawing money from an ATM and paying a surcharge. Or buying too many groceries (and then throwing a lot away) because you worry that you won't have enough food and your family will go hungry. Or drinking too much alcohol after work on Friday nights. Or maybe it's just that mobile phone plan that you

know isn't very good but that you still pay each month. In my case, it is chocolate and treats at the work cafe, and for a long time it was sugar-enriched chai latte. The little spending habits repeat themselves, and all add up.

5. **The miracle of compound interest means there are huge advantages to starting to save early and consistently.** Superannuation, in particular, is specially designed to maximise regular saving over the long term, especially now that there is an annual cap on super contributions. Investment involves time and money, and just like a big tree, it starts with something small.

6. **You develop 'value thinking' and can make good choices on large-ticket purchases when you understand that every dollar counts.** It is easy to think that you don't need to negotiate hard on big items because you can get bamboozled by big numbers. For example, Neil and I recently bought an investment property, and I negotiated hard (in a friendly and professional way) to knock a final $1000 off the purchase price. It was tempting to think that another thousand dollars or two doesn't matter because the overall price is in the hundreds of thousands, and it's all tax deductible. But I stopped and told myself that an extra thousand dollars equated to 20 weeks of groceries for my kids and me. Or, to put it another way, it is nearly half a years' worth of food and groceries. Value thinking gives you perspective.

7. **You are more likely to identify structural problems in your budget when you focus on both the big and the small.** Every month I prepare an income/expenses report. Every month I look at the same set of figures. And occasionally when I look at the figures, I realise that the choices I'm making don't make sense. For example, why am I going without coffees or teas from the cafe at work while I am paying money

on credit card fees and charges? My low-interest card still had a $49 per annum fee, on top of credit card charges, which added up to about half a cup of coffee at the cafe a week. (When I worked that out, I immediately cancelled my card.) Or why am I paying $60 a month for an online subscription that I can read at work for free? Or if my budget is so tight, why don't I get a flatmate or list my spare room on Airbnb to get some extra income? I often discover that I don't recognise the big things that are staring me in the face until I focus on the same figures again and again.

A DOLLAR SAVED IS MORE THAN A DOLLAR

Another way of demonstrating how every dollar counts is by considering the simple proposition that a dollar saved is usually more significant than a dollar earned.

Think about how hard you must work to earn the money you make. How much do you make an hour? $20? $35? What is your annual salary if you break it down into the hours that you actually work? Are you performing a lot of unpaid overtime? How much time and energy are you really putting into your job?

If you analyse your work from this perspective, that one dollar earned is not really one dollar. You pay taxes on that dollar — more if you are on a high salary due to Australia's income tax structure. You might have to pay for buses or trains to get to work (unless you have flexible working arrangements that allow you to work from home — but even then there are hidden extras with time and use of personal equipment). You might even have to buy a car just to get to work if there are no good public transport options, and then pay for petrol and parking.

It doesn't end there. You probably need to spend money on suitable work clothes to look the part (unless you have a cool high-tech job where you can lounge around in jeans or can work from home in pyjamas—Neil is a technical officer and only owns one suit, which he has never worn to work). You probably spend more than you would at home on things like coffees and takeaway lunches. Then there are work lunches and presents for colleagues who are leaving or getting married or promoted or whatever.

If you deduct all of those transport and incidental expenses from your earnings, you will find that your one dollar of earnings is much less than a dollar.

But one dollar saved can be more than a dollar, especially if you use it to invest or pay down debt. The interest rate on my mortgage is currently at a super-low rate of 3.64 per cent. If I pay one dollar off my mortgage, my $1 is worth at least $1.04. And that doesn't take into account the interest saved over the course of the loan if you repay it early. For example, if I paid off a 25-year mortgage in one year, there would be huge interest savings.

Just try crunching some numbers yourself to work out what an extra $1 a month could mean over the course of your mortgage or other debt. There are a few different online calculators. I like the ones at the Australian Government's moneysmart.gov.au website. There is also a great mortgage motivator at getmoneywise.com.au. There are many variables, so it is difficult to say conclusively that $1 equals a certain amount. That said, it certainly does matter.

What if you had a credit card debt? Many people do. The average rate is around 14.25 per cent, but many people are paying over 20 per cent, even up to 24.99 per cent. If you paid an extra dollar on your credit card debt, that dollar over the course of a year would effectively amount to between $1.14 and $1.25. (That's assuming you pay off the credit card debt within one year—many people don't.)

And what if you invested that dollar? Say you put it into index funds, shares or a high-interest-bearing account that (assuming all went well) returned at least five per cent a year. Your $1 would become $1.05 in the first year. Imagine if that investment returned ten per cent or more—then your $1 would become $1.10.

And then there is compound interest. If, every month, you added $1 to that initial $1, at the end of the year, would it equal $12? No. Assuming five per cent interest, you would have earned a whole extra dollar, and your investment would be worth $13. If you invested $1 a month for ten years, your dollar would be worth $157, and you would have earned $36 in interest. Once you have a decent mass of savings in place, the compound interest will look after itself.

Of course, once you realise an investment (i.e. sell it) you do have to pay taxes. And if you spend it, it is gone. But in general, one dollar saved is so much more than one dollar earned.

The idea is to focus on the small things in a mindful way so that the trickle of single dollars becomes a vast ocean of abundance. As they say, a journey of a thousand miles begins with a single step. So, too, your millionaire or billionaire savings journey begins with your first dollar saved.

MICRO-INVESTING

The discussion about the power of every dollar saved is not just academic. There are a number of investment products, predominantly aimed at younger millennials, that are geared at encouraging saving by starting with small amounts.

Acorns is an investment app that was founded in California by father–son team Walter and Jeff Cruttenden. It now has an Australian investment arm, which was renamed Raiz in 2018. Raiz is a platform that enables micro-investing into exchange traded funds. It is a clever idea because it enables you to get into investing with little start-up capital and low fees.

When I first heard about Raiz, I was intrigued but I didn't see a need for it. That was until Neil started staying over. Each night he would empty his pocket of spare change into a bowl. Over time, the coins filled up the bowl.

'That's a lot of money,' I said one day. 'What do you plan to do with it?'

'Well, not much to be honest,' he replied. 'Usually I just let it sit and after a year or so I might take it to the bank.'

That got me thinking: there must be a better way to use that money. Then I remembered reading some posts by other money bloggers about Raiz, so I decided to investigate.

Raiz is super-easy to set up and use, and the app is interactive. I think of it as kind of Tinder for investors. I find it oddly addictive. I love logging onto the app and seeing how things add up, and it has been a great way for me to demonstrate to Neil how quickly our little savings can multiply.

Raiz is not the only micro-investing product available. There are others including Spareship Voyager (a similar product), Carrott (aimed at encouraging small savings into superannuation), Brickx (facilitating investment into real estate), Stake (investment into US assets) and Ratesetter (peer to peer lending). I think Raiz is a particularly good introductory portal for young people or new savers to get into investing because it is easy to use and install. It also has short and focused emails that give updates about Raiz and investing in general. It is an excellent way to appreciate the value of compound interest and investing.

Of course, like any form of investment, there are risks. A Raiz investment has a higher profile of risk than a high-interest bank account, especially if the bank account is with a bank that has a savings guarantee. And you do need to have at least a few hundred dollars in the Raiz account for the $1.25 a month fee to be more competitive than a bank account with no or low fees. However, assuming the market performs well, on average it is likely to bring you better returns than leaving your money in a bank account.

Neil and I started using Raiz to save for our wedding. We opened our account with the money in Neil's coin bowl—that came to $70. I took the coins and transferred $70 from my bank account into Raiz.

I now put into Raiz the equivalent of any loose change I find lying around—I put the coins in my purse and transfer the same amount into Raiz. I also add to that any money I save (e.g. if I choose not to buy a coffee or tea at the work cafe) and the proceeds from decluttering around the house (e.g. I sold some unwanted camping stuff that was taking up space for $30, and sold a desk for $50). Neil has also been putting unspent travel allowance into the fund and we have earned around $20.33 from Raiz Rewards (a loyalty scheme where brands pay money into your Raiz account if you shop with them).

After six months, we had around $1800 in Raiz, which included $5.36 of reinvested dividends, $13.75 from market returns, $20.33 from Raiz Rewards and $5 from referrals.

RECORDING YOUR SPENDING

For over a decade I have recorded every dollar I spend. Every. Single. Dollar. Well, sometimes I miss a bit here and there. But not often.

You might wonder what the point of recording your spending is. Maybe you think it takes too much time. Or you might think it is too controlling. Or perhaps that I am just a little too obsessive and strange when it comes to money.

For years I used a free pocket diary that I got from my credit union to record my spending. Later I splurged on a $2 diary from a discount store. Now I use an app called Goodbudget. There are plenty of apps around that can help you track your spending, including more sophisticated ones like YNAB (You Need A Budget). ASIC'S MoneySmart website has developed TrackMySpend, an app that helps you distinguish between a need and a want. The essential thing is to find a system that works for you.

Recording your spending—each and every item—is important if you want to get ahead financially. If you can't commit to doing it for a decade, just try it for a week. Let me explain why it's so important.

FIVE REASONS TO RECORD YOUR SPENDING

1. **It increases your mindfulness.** Mindfulness—that buzz word that everyone is talking about. Recording your spending really does increase your mindfulness because it forces you to focus your attention on what you are doing or what you have just done. It is so easy, these days, to just 'tap and go' to pay for whatever you want. You don't even need to use cash! When you stop to record your spending, it gives you the opportunity to pause and contemplate how the experience was for you. Did you really enjoy that $4 cup of coffee? Did you taste it? Was it a spiritual experience that was the highlight of your day? Or did it taste like lukewarm dishwater? Did you really want it at all or were you just buying one because that's what you do every morning (and afternoon)?

2. **It is easy to leak money if you don't record it.** You probably know that feeling of getting to the end of the week or month and wondering where all the money went. Much of our money goes on the small, discretionary purchases that we make every day. The tiny optional splurges we don't need that are not life-saving. Like those yummy baked goods at my work cafe—I love buying from there, but often I am not hungry and only snacking to get a short mental breather from stresses at work. When I force myself to write down what I spend my money on, at the end of the month I know where it has all gone.

3. **It provides essential data for your budget.** Budget: that dirty word that many of us fear. At the end of each month, I add up my income

and expenses and put it in a spreadsheet. It is my moment of truth. I recently used this data to formulate a budget. There's no point saying I live on bread and water and only go out for dinner once a year as I would be lying to myself. Having reliable data is essential to allow me to see how much I spend on things like groceries, petrol and dining out. Recording expenses helps identify trends (like the fact that I spend a lot at the work cafe, and that I have a bit of an op shop addiction).

4. **It makes you accountable for your spending.** It's a bit like going on a diet — if you don't own what really goes into your mouth versus what you think you eat, you aren't going to be able to stick to a diet. (Yes, a bit of a wellness theme here that points to my weaknesses.) Writing down what you spend holds you accountable.

5. **The mega-wealthy know where their money goes — every single dollar.** I recently reread Thomas J. Stanley and William D. Danko's *The Millionaire Next Door: The Surprising Secrets of America's Wealthy.* It contains a whole chapter about how wealthy people — genuine, mega-wealthy people — track their money. They know exactly where their money is going, and they spend a lot of time recording it. Many of them are at the stage that they no longer need to do this, yet they still do so. Wealthy people are organised and value every single dollar.

FINANCIALLY FREE

Not long after I began working for the public service, I went to see a financial planner.

'Based on the average retirement age of 65, you will work another 37 years,' he said.

'Nooooooo!' I remember silently screaming. Thirty-seven years seemed like a very long time.

WHERE HAVE MY SAVINGS GONE?
AND HOW TO START AGAIN FROM SCRATCH

A good friend of mine, Michelle Taylor, photographer at Kazuri Photography and blogger at Dory the Explorer, allowed me to share her savings and spending experience. I think it speaks to why small decisions are really important, and why every dollar counts. I had previously admired Michelle's focus and commitment (and her creative use of sausages) in saving for a family holiday overseas (the photos were stunning). I was thus surprised to learn that Michelle had encountered some significant savings challenges since arriving back in Australia. Here is Michelle's story:

This time last year my bank statement looked rather impressive as far as my savings were concerned. I don't consider myself to be a big spender, especially if there is the promise of travel looming, so the accumulation of funds slowly built and I gave myself a mental pat on the back.

Then one morning I looked online, and there was barely any money in my account! I panicked; had I been robbed, had my card been stolen? A frantic scan of my statements revealed that the only thief of my funds was myself. Without even thinking about it, I had drained away my savings.

The first culprit I noticed was the leeching buys, those small, painless (well, painless at the time) purchases of a coffee here or a cheap fast food snack there; buying everyone a smoothie when we were out shopping; buying a book rather than borrowing it from the library. Impulse buys, hangry buys; all those little purchases added up.

And then, quite uncharacteristic for me, were the big purchases of 2017. Two expensive new lenses sat in my camera case; the accommodation for a family reunion was not cheap; an expensive yet worthwhile splurge of a girls' weekend to Melbourne for my daughter and myself (plane tickets, staying at a nice hotel, eating out and seeing a show); not to mention forking out big bucks to produce a calendar that turned out to be unsellable. Oh, and Christmas. Argh!

So, with a plan to be in the air in just 11 months, I found myself saving from scratch. How was this going to happen?

Well, for one thing, never underestimate the zeal of wanderlust. I can already feel the steely focus of money-saving ZEAL beginning to course through my veins, fortifying me against the traps of good coffee, ready-made meals and fun outings trying to seduce the dollars from my wallet. The ZEAL helps!

And maybe the fact that the trip is now a short-term goal rather than a long-term one will make it easier to save hard. Doing without some of those luxuries, sticking to that bread and water diet essential to a pre-trip budget when the big reward is dangling so tantalisingly close will seem less of a chore, I hope.

I will be buying nothing this year that is not essential. That is the goal. No camera equipment, no teaching resources, no clothes, hair appointments or silly grocery buys. If it does happen, if I do slip, I will do a post of shame. The older kids have their own money so they will be buying their own junk food and fast food (although I will provide the 12-year-old with one fast food meal a fortnight).

The need to save money forces me to put my photography skills out there a little more. I have a couple of weddings, an event and some family shoots coming up in the next few weeks, and because I have had a few jobs in the past month, I am feeling excited and in the zone. Plus, the ZEAL makes me really brave!

Since sharing this, with commitment and discipline, Michelle's wealth is growing. And she did manage to save the money she needed for her family adventure. (I should add that the wedding photos she took to earn extra money are absolutely amazing.)

I was enjoying my new job, for which I had studied for many years. I found it fulfilling, interesting and at times glamorous. But did I want to be tied to it for the next 37 years before I could retire? No way.

Most financial planners are focused on the idea of working until you retire. The idea is an old-fashioned one: you work in a stable job for many years, get your golden handshake, sit around on your sofa for a few years and then die.

These days, people are living longer. And they are having multiple career changes, in part because the nature of work has changed. They may even work multiple jobs at the same time. Holding down a job where you go to a factory or an office is a bit of an industrial revolution construct. Already people are able to work from home, or earn money driving an Uber, doing jobs via AirTasker or tapping away at their computers doing digital projects.

I know many younger people who don't want to be working until they turn 65 or older. They want to be free before they are 40, or even earlier.

I prefer the term 'financially free' to 'retirement'. Being financially free means that you have enough money coming in to give you the freedom to leave your job at any time if you want to, and also that you are free to pivot to another occupation.

There are good reasons for staying in a job, including the social dimension and feeling like you are making a difference—working isn't just about money. However, if you are not financially free you might be tied to working in a job whether or not you like it. Perhaps you are being bullied at work (depressingly common), or in a job you thought you should do rather than being able to follow your passion. For example, you might be working as a medical professional but dream of being an actor. If you are financially free, you are more likely to be able to take risks, such as dropping to part-time work while you start acting classes.

'Retirement' suggests that you suddenly stop. I have many retired friends and family, and few of them have done that. Some have started new 'work' as volunteers in their community, some have travelled the world and then worked again for a while before 'retiring' again, and others have started new businesses. My friends Dan and Maureen Etherington, for instance, pioneered an innovation for extracting coconut oil as Dan was retiring as a lecturer. Their company Kokonut Pacific now sells coconut oil through its niulife brand in Australia and internationally. It's not the retirement they expected.

When you are starting out in your career, or even working part-time when you are studying, you might not think that small savings add up. However, just like a squirrel who begins preparing for winter by gathering acorns, it is important to start saving away bits and pieces well before the time comes when you want to leave work. The earlier you start, the sooner you can be financially free to live the life of your dreams.

FRUGALISTA CHALLENGE

Your challenge is to record every cent that you spend for a month. You can write this in a diary, use a phone app, create a spreadsheet or use the lined pages at the end of this book. It doesn't matter as long as you record your expenses honestly.

At the end of the month, review what you spent. Were the purchases on things like takeaway food, coffees, clothes or going out worth what you spent on them? Is there anything that surprised you about your spending?

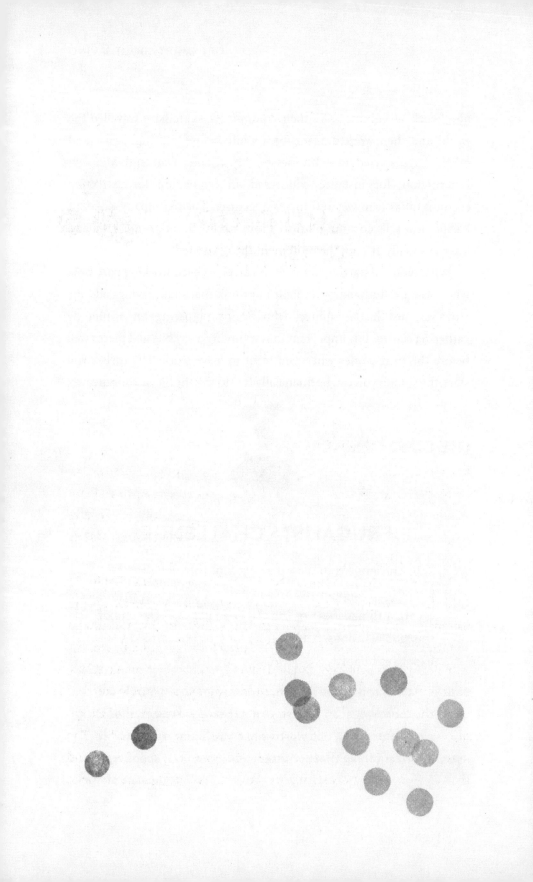

CHAPTER 3

LIGHT UP
FOR LESS

Saving on energy

THE COST OF ENERGY

In Canberra where I live, electricity prices went up by 20 per cent on 1 July 2017 and sneaked up again in 2018. This amounted to an extra $579 per year on average for most households. Prices in other states and territories also went up, by $379 on average in New South Wales, $488 in South Australia and $192 in Queensland for AGL Energy.

Meanwhile, according to the Australian Energy Regulator (AER), in 2017 the Australian Capital Territory had the highest annual gas bill nationally, with median bills double that of those in Queensland and $500 more than in South Australia. We use a lot of gas in Canberra.

Before you feel too sorry for me, I should point out that the electricity tariff in Canberra is one of the lowest in Australia, and nearly half that of nearby New South Wales. However, we do feel the pinch of energy prices in Canberra owing to extremes in cold and hot weather. The heaters are traditionally turned on around Anzac Day on 25 April and they stay on almost constantly for the next six months. In summer, temperatures soar into the high 30s and sometimes they will hit or even exceed 40°C.

The trend of rising electricity prices is likely to continue, and the issue of energy is a hot topic. In 2017, Australia's Chief Scientist, Dr Alan Finkel, delivered a review into energy (also known as the Finkel Review), and the Government responded by adopting 49 of the 50 recommendations and proposing a National Energy Guarantee (NEG) instead. The disagreement over the NEG within the coalition government led to Malcolm Turnbull losing his position as Prime Minister. Energy policy is that politically sensitive, and I feel it is likely to be this way for some time.

Lower income families are already feeling pressure. The AER reported that in Queensland more people had their power disconnected in 2017 than any other state or territory. Meanwhile, South Australia had the highest proportion of electricity customers in debt, with five out of every 100 residential customers holding an average debt level of $1596. Rising energy costs could also impact in other ways, such as increasing refrigeration costs in supermarkets, which will push up the price of key food items as a consequence.

What can you do about all of this? Be empowered. This chapter provides some tips and tricks to help you make big savings in your energy costs. Many of the tips will also help reduce carbon emissions, thereby helping the environment as well. Describing yourself as an environmental warrior sounds much cooler than saying you're a cheapskate and want to spend less on electricity and gas.

I've based the calculations in this chapter on peak residential rates offered by ActewAGL for Canberra customers as of June 2018, i.e. 26.08 cents/kilowatt hour (kWh). Canberra has some of the lowest rates of electricity in Australia. For some areas in New South Wales, you may need to double these figures. For other states or territories, refer to the pricing of your energy provider.

The first step is to work out how much you are paying for energy. Doing this is important as many people have no idea what is on their power bills—I certainly had no idea before I started to examine the issue of energy usage. I did not budget for it, I was in denial about it, and I had no idea how to read my bill.

I remember how scary it was each time I got my energy bill in my old house. My four-bedroom house with a granny flat was a 1970s-style Canberra brick home that had not been well insulated, and even though we had added insulation, there is only so much you can do retrospectively. I had flatmates and a tenant in the granny flat, and I paid energy costs for the lot. It is hard to tell people not to use electricity, especially when they are cold. I am now in a smaller and well-insulated apartment, but my energy bill remains high.

I encourage you to find your electricity bill (and gas bill, if you have both connected) for this time last year. If you don't have one, you can contact your energy company to request a copy. If you are busy and don't have a lot of time, keep reading and do this step later.

CALCULATING YOUR ENERGY COSTS

1. **Take your electricity bill and divide the cost by the number of days in the bill (e.g. 90 days if it's a quarterly bill).** Ideally, do this for the entire year—add up all four bills and divide the total by 365, which will give you a figure for what you pay *per day* for electricity.

2. **Do the same for gas, if you have it connected.** Add the two amounts together to work out your daily energy cost.

3. **Look at your energy usage to see if your overall usage is increasing or decreasing over time.** Pay attention to your usage over the same time period each year.

4. Write down your calculations so you have a reference point. This will enable you to see how much you are going to save.

I find it useful to think in terms of what you are paying per day for electricity and gas. Otherwise, it's easy to dismiss how the little things we do daily can make a difference. Every time you turn on the lights, the heater, the oven or the television, there is a cost. Every time you turn something on in your house, you are deciding how you use energy.

When I lived in my four-bedroom house with a granny flat (and ducted gas heating), the total electricity and gas cost for 12 months, from May 2016 to February 2017, was $4247.34, or $11.63 per day. This doesn't include the 20 per cent price increase in July 2017 — if I had stayed in that house, my annual bill would have grown by $509 to $4757.02, or $13.03 per day.

I felt shocked when I saw the results of these sums. During much of this time, I was doing a $50 a week grocery challenge, so I was effectively paying over $3 more for heating each day than I was paying for food and groceries. I had no idea that I was throwing so much away on heating and cooling costs. I am paying almost a quarter less in energy costs in my new apartment. Over the last year, the cost of electricity was $1323.97 for four people, which amounted to $3.63 per day. We were cosy, but there is room for improvement with more cost-saving measures.

WHAT TO DO IF YOU CANNOT PAY YOUR ENERGY BILL

In the unhappy event that you or someone you know is struggling to pay an electricity or gas bill, don't despair. Maybe you got hit by a larger bill than expected and don't know where to find the money to pay it. Or maybe you suddenly lost your job and are struggling to pay. I like to focus on the positives, about building abundance and investing wisely, so I hope you won't find yourself in this situation. However,

I know many Australians do struggle to pay their energy bills at times, particularly in winter and summer.

The main thing not to do is to suffer in the cold (or sweltering heat) in silence. If you are struggling to pay your bills, speak to your energy provider. It's easy to think that energy companies are hard-hearted, faceless corporate entities making money from little people at any cost. Most are privatised, and yes, they are in the business of making money. However, they also have tips on how to save money and reduce costs. In some cases, they also provide financial support.

Most energy providers have policies to allow for times when people are experiencing hardship. For instance, ActewAGL in Canberra has a hardship policy that involves working with people to set up flexible and affordable payment plans, and ensuring that electricity remains connected through its Staying Connected program. Yes, if you fess up about the problem, they won't turn off your electricity in the middle of a cold winter night. ActewAGL has invested $250,000 in creating an Energy Support Fund, which includes a dedicated bill hotline. It also works with community groups that provide services to people who are struggling. For example, sometimes community groups hand out energy vouchers.

NEGOTIATE THE BEST POSSIBLE DEAL WITH YOUR ENERGY RETAILER

Did you know that you can negotiate a better deal on your electricity bill? Surprisingly, some people don't know that you can do this, even though there is a Federal Government campaign to ensure that energy companies pass on the best rates to consumers. The campaign was even championed by former Prime Minister Malcom Turnbull, who urged consumers to negotiate better deals and energy retailers to make better deals available.

Perhaps you first got your electricity and gas connected when you moved into your house many years ago. Do you keep paying the bill quarterly? Do you assume that you do not have any other options? Even if you have a contract in place, you can switch before the end of the contract. It might mean you have to pay a small exit fee, but if you are getting a better rate, the costs could be worth it.

There are now more and more energy retailers on the market, and this is set to increase. There is talk of telecommunication companies entering the energy utility space, and even motoring associations such as NRMA are now providing energy plans. More entrants mean that you have increasingly more choice — and more bargaining power.

The first step is often to negotiate the best possible deal with your existing energy retailer. Call them and ask to speak to someone in the sales area. Be polite and persistent (they are likely to transfer you to a few people before you get the right area).

I suggest using this script: 'Hi. My name is [insert name here]. I have an electricity/gas account with you. I am researching options and comparing products. I am wondering if I currently have the best deal with you.'

When I tried this with my energy retailer, I felt so nervous. I thought they were going to laugh at me. They transferred me three times and then there was a pause before someone said, 'Certainly, we can help you by offering you a 12-month contract with a 12 per cent discount.'

'Yes, please,' I said.

Thankfully my apartment is well insulated and does not use much electricity compared with my previous house, but for me that discount still worked out at an annual saving of around $148.32. Not bad for one phone call and less than half an hour of my time.

Several people I know have since tried this technique, including my dad. I was surprised that he asked me for advice, but not surprised that he secured a discount. He received 34 per cent off his electricity bill, so for one quarter he paid $309 rather than $468—a saving of $159 a quarter. Assuming similar usage throughout the year, this is an annual saving of $636.

COMPARE PRODUCTS

In most urban areas in Australia, there are numerous energy retailers to choose from. How do you know if you are getting the best value for the service you require?

In response to concerns about rising energy costs for consumers, the Government established the Energy Made Easy website (energymadeeasy. gov.au), which is an online price comparison tool from the Australian Energy Regulator (AER).

Using the website is easy. You are prompted to put in some key details such as your postcode (your location will determine which companies you have access to), which products you want to compare (electricity and/or gas), the dates on your last bill and the rates you are currently being charged. If you have your latest bill in front of you, this should be straightforward.

The website then, based on the data you give, offers a series of options for products that would offer you a lower rate. In Canberra, we do not have as many choices as other urban areas. That said, the market has been deregulated since late 2017, and there is now more than one energy provider. While I am on the best available deal at the moment, I will be monitoring this site frequently to see if I can get an even better one.

SET UP A DIRECT DEBIT ARRANGEMENT

Do you wait until your utility bill is due, then scramble to find money to pay it? If you set up a direct debit instead, you might even get a discount.

My energy retailer, ActewAGL, offers a direct debit system called Even Pay. Your yearly utility bill is averaged out into fortnightly chunks, and you receive a 5c discount each week, which works out to a saving of $20 per year. That might not sound like a lot, but I can buy a lot of food for $20 — almost half a week's groceries if I need to. Remember, the little savings all add up.

The big saving, though, is in being able to budget your bills better so that you don't get hit with any nasty surprises, especially in late winter or early spring. Further, you get to know per fortnight (and thus per day) what your utility costs are, and this can help you be more mindful of your electricity usage.

However, you could be better off paying your bills as they arrive. You might not think about it when you receive your bill, but it is a blessing to receive electricity, gas and water and only be billed for it three months later. You need to pay rent in advance (and pay bond as well), but with utilities, you use and pay later. You are effectively getting three months interest-free use of such utilities. If you have enough savings to be able to weather each bill, then ActewAGL also offers a discount if you set up the 'Full Pay' option so that your bills are paid from your nominated bank account automatically.

EMBRACE THE APRÈS-SKI LIFESTYLE

My non-frugal hobby is skiing. My dad used to take my sister and me when we were young, and I just loved the whole experience. It was tough at times and cold, but we were rewarded with magnificent mountain views, the exhilaration of flying down the slopes and, at the end of the day, a chalet with a fireplace and fantastic winter food — stews, apple strudels, mulled wine and so on. A few years ago, I took up the hobby again, and we now budget for a short skiing trip to nearby Perisher each year.

I often wonder why more people don't think of their home as a chalet. How could you make your home warm and cosy? How could you accept the cold that goes with winter as something positive, as a celebration of the season? Why do we put up with snow and wind on a chairlift, but freak out when we need to walk down the street in the cold?

Having the heaters on full bore is obviously expensive, but there are fun ways you can celebrate winter in the home. For example, by putting candles on the table, cooking hearty meals, wearing your favourite winter woollies (or ponchos), having cuddles on the couch and movie nights. Or rug up and head out to explore favourite cafes with fireplaces.

The Germans have a term for this winter cosiness: *gemütlich*. I remember a school exchange trip to Germany when I was in high school. We would spend Sunday afternoons at home, listening to Beethoven, eating black forest cake or stollen, drinking coffee or mulled wine, playing chess or baking *plätzchen* (Christmas cookies). My homestay mother taught me how to knit woollen socks as well. Perhaps it doesn't sound as exciting as extreme winter sports, but it was a lot of fun, and it celebrated the season of winter.

One way that you can celebrate the winter season is through warm winter pyjamas, aka winter flannies. Do you own a pair of flannelette pyjamas? If so, do you wear them in winter? I do, and I love them. On arctic days here in Canberra, such as the coldest weekend in 20 years celebrated in July 2017 (colder than Thredbo), my kids and I hung out in our flannies nearly all day. My kids, who are of the generation that are chauffeured from one after-school activity to yet another, rejoiced in the idea of staying home relaxing on a cold day in their flannies. In fact, they begged me to allow them to do it again. We had porridge for breakfast, played board games, watched TV, did some baking together (actually, I did most of it) and just relaxed.

One of my Taiwanese friends, who is a practitioner of Traditional Chinese Medicine, said that it is natural for us to slow down in winter.

Animals in the wild go into full or partial hibernation. It follows that it is quite okay for humans to take it easy when the weather is cold as well. I do like hitting the slopes, and I have been cycling in the cold weather, but for the most part, I like to relax and hang out in my flannies—hot water bottle optional.

DRAUGHT-PROOFING YOUR HOME

So, you're all rugged up and enjoying your après-ski life. But then cold air sneaks into your house, making it feel much colder than the thermostat is telling you it is. What can you do about it? Insulate!

Apart from making your home more comfortable, one of my friends said she saved 30 per cent on her heating bill by insulating her house. With many people having energy bills of $4000 or more a year, this is a saving of over $1000.

Improved insulation in your ceiling, and even in your walls, can significantly help prevent heat loss from your home. It can be expensive, but look around for the occasional government-backed energy efficiency scheme that can help offset some of the costs. Newer housing generally has better insulation as most building codes make energy efficient/green housing mandatory.

If you have lots of money and a status home with spectacular views, you might see the value in double glazing. Double glazing will enhance the aesthetic value of your home, so that you can feel like you're in a cosy mountain lodge looking out at the sunset or the fairy lights below. It will dramatically reduce the heat loss in your home, but if you have large windows, it will come at a cost that probably will not be worth it in terms of energy savings. Simply put: install double glazing if you want to look out through your windows on a winter night without feeling cold, but otherwise there are cheaper (if perhaps less aesthetically pleasing) options.

Neil and I recently went to a free energy-saving workshop that was delivered by Lish Fejer (aka Australia's Queen of Green). Lish blogs at greenityourself.com.au about sustainability, including some easy and cheap ways to insulate your home, even if it is a rental home. She is ever so funny and had Neil and I in stitches with her stories of insulating on the cheap. Check out Lish's blog for a host of DIY insulation ideas.

Here are some key steps you can take to insulate your home:

- **Use a mozzie coil to discover draughts.** You might be surprised where the air is getting in. Light a mozzie coil and walk around the house to reveal any draughts.

- **Cover up ventilation holes with clear adhesive plastic book covering.** Sometimes homes have had ventilation specially installed. You can cover these up in winter with clear adhesive book covering. (Ensure you allow for adequate ventilation if you are using gas or kerosene for heating, to prevent the risk of poisoning.)

- **Fill up draught holes.** Start with the biggest hole and the cheapest form of tape or hole filler — use foam pool noodles if you have to. Then gradually work in with more specialised (and more expensive) tape.

- **Use a double-sided door snake.** Yes, this exists and is an example of good Australian ingenuity. It covers both sides of the door, and you do not have to remember to kick it out of the way when you open the door.

- **Cover exhaust fans with draught stoppers.** Invented in Albury–Wodonga, these contraptions prevent hot or cold air entering through your exhaust fan. They cost around $30 and will save you hundreds of dollars in heating or cooling.

- **Bubble wrap large expanses of windows.** Yes, bubble wrapping inside your house is a thing and there are YouTube videos showing how to install it. Not only is this cheaper than double glazing, but you can easily take it off in summer. The bubble wrap sticks to the window with water and is easy to remove.

- **Install curtains or blinds with pelmets on top.** Quality curtains with pelmets on top can dramatically decrease heat loss in your home. It is important that your curtains fit properly, without any large gaps that allow cool air to come through and heat to escape. The basic rule is that as soon as the sun goes down, draw the curtains. It's a waste of energy to have a heater running while the curtains are open.

Note that when you insulate your home, it is important that you also ventilate it. Ventilation is important to prevent mould and mildew, which are caused by condensation, and also to prevent fatal poisoning from gas fumes. You may need to open windows during the day to allow air to flow while you are at work. A good friend splurged on expensive curtains, only to find that they were attacked by mould due to the large amounts of condensation that built up on her windows. Think about ventilation before you invest in designer curtains! In bad cases, where there is insufficient ventilation, condensation can be so bad that it causes timber window frames to buckle. The best way to avoid that is to both ventilate your home and wipe down your windows each morning.

SEEING THE LIGHT

The electric light bulb has often been hailed as one of the single greatest inventions in modern society. Whether it was Thomas Edison's idea or, as some people maintain, he stole it from Nikola Tesla, my light bulb moment actually came from Neil.

Neil is a good man. He's a keeper. He visited my house a few times before we were dating, and one time he arrived with new energy-efficient LED lights in hand. He proceeded — unasked — to change nearly all my light bulbs to ones with a lower wattage that were more energy efficient.

'It just made sense,' he said later. 'You had all these old inefficient halogens installed.'

To be honest, I had no idea what type of lights I had installed. They were downlight things. They worked, albeit slowly. I had no idea what the difference was, and I did not think it was much.

Each 4-Watt LED downlight that Neil installed for me would cost $1.14 per year to run for three hours a day at 26.08c/kWh. By comparison, a 15-Watt compact fluorescent tube downlight would cost $4.28 per year. And the 52-Watt halogen downlights I had were each costing me $14.85 per year. Neil replaced eight halogen downlights with LED downlights, which would only cost $9.12 a year to run. The eight halogens had been costing me $118.80 a year to run.

Neil saved me around $109.68 a year just by swapping eight halogen downlights for LEDs. A four-pack of LED downlights costs around $30 at Woolworths or $12 at Costco. So, assuming he purchased the eight LED lights from Costco, they would cost $24 and represent a saving of approximately $85.68 in the first year. If you lived in another state and were paying a higher rate for your electricity, you would save even more.

In 2016, ActewAGL changed the light bulbs in my previous house to LED *for free*. It was part of a program it ran to promote energy efficiency. Unfortunately, it no longer runs that program for home usage. However, it is worth checking with your local energy retailer to investigate whether they are offering any similar schemes.

Another thing to consider is heat lamps in bathrooms (who doesn't love these in winter?). Each heat bulb is 250 Watts and a bathroom usually has a double unit that is 500 Watts. Assuming you use them for

30 minutes a day, each unit would cost around $22.40 a year to run. Of course, if you have teenagers who spend hours in the bathroom or if you have young kids (like I do) who forget to turn them off… you get the drift. Best to turn off these heat lamps when not in use. They are only effective when you are standing directly under them, so they don't do much when you are directly under the shower in any case.

SHORTER SHOWERS CAN DRASTICALLY REDUCE YOUR POWER BILL

Australia is the driest continent on earth, and many of us are aware of the need to conserve water. But did you know that heating hot water in your home can contribute to up to 25 per cent of your energy bill?

Yes, that's right: *a quarter of your energy bill* probably goes in hot water heating costs. If you have a few teenagers in the household, it might even be more.

One of the most cost-effective ways of reducing this expenditure is to avoid showering so much. If you think about it, why do we need to shower every day? If you are out doing physical labour then clearly there is a need, but what about if you are sitting in an office? What about in winter? I often find that my skin gets dry and itchy if I bathe too often in winter. In Taiwan when I followed the traditional month-long post-baby confinement, I didn't step into the shower or wash my hair for a month (disclaimer: I did have sponge baths, and I did use dry shampoo—I did not ignore personal hygiene!). In Japan, people usually have a quick shower then use a shared bath, which is another option, especially if you have young kids. Couples could economise on showers by taking them together (just saying).

Alternatively, you could do what I am doing at present and cycle to work and use the shower facilities in the change room. Not only am I saving money, I am getting fit and reducing carbon emissions as well.

Technically anyone could use the shower facilities, whether or not they are cycling or exercising, but it does feel a bit dishonest to use the hot water just because it's free.

If you have teenagers who need a reminder about how long they are spending in the shower, take this tip from a friend of mine. She installed a waterproof shower timer, with strict instructions that it was to be used for four-minute showers. There are many different models available, some for under $5.

You could also shower to a favourite song—most songs are around four minutes, but the challenge, if you're using your phone, is to make sure your screen doesn't lock before the time's up. Yes, I have had my favourite song end mid-way through.

These days it's trendy to have large showerheads that spew out a lot of water so that you feel like raindrops keep falling on your head. The problem is that they use up a lot of water. You can buy a simple water flow disc for around $5, which helps to reduce water usage without restricting the feel of your rain shower. The savings can be quite amazing.

I was curious to know how much it cost to have a shower in terms of the energy used. So Neil did some calculations for me, shown in the table over the page. First, check the flow rate of your shower by using a bucket to catch the water over one minute.

ELECTRICITY COSTS OF SHOWERING

	Water flow disc 9 litres/minute		Water-saver shower head 13 litres/minute		Unrestricted shower head 21 litres/minute	
Shower time	5 min	10 min	5 min	10 min	5 min	10 min
Water used by 2 people for 1 shower each per day	90 litres	180 litres	130 litres	260 litres	210 litres	420 litres
Cost per day	$1.59	$3.18	$2.297	$4.594	$3.71	$7.42
Cost per year	$580.35	$1160.70	$838.40	$1676.81	$1354.15	$2708.30

*Costs based on electricity rate of 26.08c/kWh using electric storage hot water system

Also be aware of leaking water heaters or water heaters that are not insulated. Often water heaters are located outside. Think how cold they would be on a −5°C morning in Canberra, and how much energy it would take for them to heat from super-cold to hot. An inspection of your water heater could be one of the most energy-efficient decisions you make in your home. Can you adjust the thermostat to a lower temperature? Could you buy and install some rubber insulation for your water pipes? Or insulate the water heater itself?

Consider also how you wash your clothes. Do you really need your clothes to be washed at super-hot temperatures? I have used cold water for years and have never experienced any problems. In fact, I think it works better for some stains that might set in hotter water. I make my own detergent (see page 74), and I never have any problems with it dissolving. According to the Alliance to Save Energy (ase.org), up to 90 per cent of the energy used to wash clothes is from heating the water, so there are big cost savings to be made by using cold water.

TURN DOWN THE HEATER AND TURN UP THE AIR CONDITIONER

You can reduce heating costs by heating yourself rather than the whole house. Put on a jumper, put on a poncho, wrap yourself in a blanket or wear a coat. Layers work well. Who cares if it is a fashion statement or not—just wear warm clothes! If you are still cold, consider using a hot water bottle. I have poor circulation and feel the cold, so I always sit with a hot water bottle on my lap in winter. Or try using a heated blanket. A model that is sometimes sold at ALDI costs $35 to buy and only around 2c an hour to run, and would keep you nice and toasty while sitting on the sofa watching Netflix. In contrast, a small bar heater would cost you 44c an hour to run.

In winter, the ideal heating setting is between 18 and 20°C. Many energy providers do not recommend putting the temperature up above 20°C. If you can live with it at 18°C, then leave it set at that. According to switchyourthinking.com, the website of South East Regional Energy Group, energy consumption rises around ten per cent for every degree above 18°C.

Do you really need the heater on overnight? I find I don't sleep well if my room is too warm. I much prefer to use a hot water bottle to snuggle up to until my bed starts to feel warm. And these days I have a partner to cuddle up to, which saves on energy heating costs!

Another way to reduce heating costs is to turn off your heater 15 to 30 minutes before you leave the house. For one thing, this minimises the chance of you forgetting to turn it off. However, the main reason is that it takes a lot of energy to heat your home. Why spend money to heat it, only to walk out the door? Turning it off 15 minutes before you leave could save an hour and 45 minutes a week in heating costs, or 157 hours of heating time over a 90-day quarter.

Watching your electricity consumption in summer is important as well. Switchyourthinking.com recommends you set your air conditioner to 24°C or warmer, as every degree cooler than this uses around ten per cent more energy. A fan uses much less energy than an air conditioner and can be effective when the weather is not too hot. Make your home as cool as a cave by closing curtains, shutting doors and shading the outside of windows as much as possible.

HOUSEHOLD APPLIANCES

Some household appliances use more energy than others. Have you ever wondered how a change in your habits at home could make a change to the bottom line in your energy usage?

To ascertain exactly how much power your plug-in appliances use, you can buy a usage meter that determines how many Watts an appliance uses. If you live in the ACT, you can borrow a smart energy kit from your local library—the ACT Government makes Home Energy Action Kits available for borrowing at ACT Public Libraries.

Spending time and money working out how much your appliances cost you to run might not be a priority for you, so I have outlined (with the help of Neil) the cost of running three common energy-intensive household items. The calculations are based on an electricity rate of 26.08c/kWh.

- **Electric kettle:** It costs 4c to boil a full jug and 1.32c to boil a jug that is filled to the minimum level. If you boiled a full jug four times a day for a year, it would cost $58.40. Boiling a minimum-filled jug four times a day for a year costs $19.27, so you could save almost $40 a year just by boiling less water. (If you do boil more water than you need, tip it into a thermos, ready for your next cup of tea or coffee.)

- **Hair dryer:** I have fine hair that gets brittle when dried with a hair dryer, so I use one infrequently. However, in many households it is considered a necessity. A hair dryer costs 8c to run for 10 minutes. Assuming you use it every day for 10 minutes, it would cost $29 a year to run (multiply that if you have more than one woman or sharply groomed man in your household).

- **Clothes dryer:** I have a dryer in my apartment, which came with the unit. I have not used it all winter and I do not intend to. Clothes dry fast enough, even in winter. In my old house, I used to place a clothes rack over a ducted heating vent and allowed the warm air to flow up onto the clothes. An average 90-minute clothes dryer cycle costs 80c to run. Assuming you used it twice a week in the three months of winter, that would add up to $19.20.

COOKING

How you cook your food can make a difference to your energy costs. It doesn't make sense to bake things like lasagne in the middle of summer while the air conditioner is cranked up full bore. Or to eat chilled foods like salad in the middle of winter when you're freezing.

It makes sense to eat food according to the seasons. In summer, you can stop your house from heating up too much by cooking food in a slow cooker outside or in your bathroom. I used to make beef stock for Vietnamese pho soup this way, or cook corned beef that I would then slice and serve as part of a simple cold salad (so retro, but when done well, so nice).

How does using an oven compare to, say, a slow cooker? For the sake of comparison, I've taken a classic Julia Childs recipe for Beef Bourguignon, and shown the cost of cooking it using five different methods (see over).

BEEF BOURGUIGNON

1 kg chuck steak or gravy beef, diced

2 rashers of bacon

2 small onions, sliced

2 tablespoons oil

1 cup (250 ml) red wine (be generous!)

1 cup (250 ml) beef stock

Button mushrooms (as many as you like)

1 tablespoon plain flour

SLOW COOKER METHOD

Fry the bacon (you will only need half the oil for this recipe). Combine all the ingredients (other than the mushrooms and flour) in the slow cooker and cook on low for 6 hours. Add the mushrooms and cook for a further 2 hours. An hour or so before serving, mix the flour with some water and stir into the stew.

Total cooking time: 8 hours
Cooking cost: 11.5c

STOVETOP METHOD

In a large cast-iron Dutch oven, brown the beef with half the oil. Transfer to a plate. Fry the onions and bacon with the remaining oil. Return the beef to the Dutch oven, cover with the red wine and beef stock and cook for 1½ hours. Add the mushrooms and cook for a further half an hour. Combine the flour with a little bit of water (and some of the cooking liquid), pour into the beef mixture and cook for around 5–10 minutes until thickened.

Total cooking time: 2½ hours on the stovetop
Cooking cost: 44.3c

OVEN METHOD

Fry the beef, onion and bacon as in the stovetop method, add the wine and stock and bake at 160°C for 2 hours. Add the mushrooms and the flour mixed with a little water and bake for another half an hour. (While the oven is on, bake a self-saucing chocolate pudding for dessert and a batch of muffins for mid-week lunches.) When finished, leave the oven door open to heat the house.

Total cooking time: 20 minutes on the stovetop,
    2½ hours in the oven
Cooking cost: 88.7c

THERMAL COOKER (OFTEN USED FOR CAMPING)

Begin as per the stovetop method, then bring to the boil for around 10 minutes until sufficiently hot. Allow to sit for 6 hours. Add the mushrooms and flour/water mixture to the casserole and allow to cook another 2–3 hours.

Total cooking time: 20 minutes on the stovetop,
    8+ hours thermal cooking (no cost)
Cooking cost: 7.8c

MICROWAVE METHOD

Microwave the bacon on high for around 1 minute, between sheets of paper towel. Coat the beef in the flour and cook on high for 5 minutes in a microwave-safe container. Combine the beef and bacon with the remaining ingredients and cook on medium for up to 55 minutes.

Total cooking time: 1 hour
Cooking cost: 16.2c

OFF-PEAK SAVINGS

Some electricity retailers provide financial incentives for consumers to use energy at times when not as many other people are using it. You can see if your company provides you with an off-peak savings benefit by looking at your electricity bill.

For instance, my energy retailer ActewAGL prices electricity as follows (as of 2 June 2018):

Peak (7–9 am and 5–8 pm): 26.08c/kWh
Shoulder (9 am–5 pm and 8–10 pm): 18.65c/kWh
Off peak (10 pm–7 am): 14.66c/kWh

As you can see, it is around 12 cents cheaper per kWh (almost half the cost) to run an appliance after 10 pm and before 7 am than at peak times. This means that you will save money if you put your dishwasher on at 10 pm as you go to bed, or program your washing machine to finish its cycle before 7 am.

Neil ran some calculations based on our Samsung front-loading 7.5 kg washing machine (it has a four-star energy rating), which uses 65 litres per wash. We usually do a cold wash to save energy heating costs, but these costs are based on a standard cotton cycle wash (which is what the machine assumes most people use).

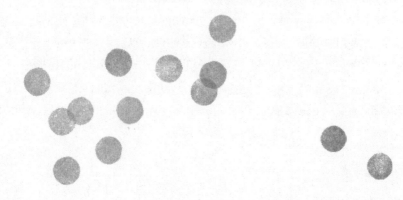

COST COMPARISONS FOR A STANDARD LOAD OF WASHING

Energy type	Wash type	Cost per wash
Peak	Cold wash	11.2c
	Warm wash (40°C)	19.6c
Shoulder	Cold wash	9.4c
	Warm wash (40°C)	13.8c
Off peak	Cold wash	6.6c
	Warm wash (40°C)	10.9c

If you did three loads of washing a week using warm water at peak times, you would spend 58.8c a week or $30.58 a year. However, if you did the washing at off-peak times rather than peak times, you would spend 32.7c a week or $17 a year—a saving of $13.57 a year.

If you just washed at off-peak times using cold water, you would spend 19.8c per week and $10.29 a year. This amounts to a saving of $20.29 a year. As you have probably noticed in this chapter, the little savings all add up—especially when you consider that a saving of $20.29 is equivalent to six days, or nearly a week, of electricity (at the rate of $3.63 per day in my apartment).

HOMEMADE WASHING POWDER

My homemade washing powder costs around $3.90. I make a double batch and it lasts me around six to eight months. You only need a tablespoon (or less) for a load, and it works in either a top- or front-loading machine.

The better the quality of soap that you use, the better the result — try to choose a brand that's labelled as 'pure' soap. You can also buy pre-grated laundry soap, but I find it is much cheaper to grate it yourself and it only takes an extra minute or two in a food processor. I use Lectric brand of washing soda.

1 bar pure soap
2 cups bicarbonate
  of soda
1 cup washing soda
Around 10 drops of
  eucalyptus oil or
  lavender oil

METHOD:

1. Grate the soap using the grater attachment of a food processor or a box grater.

2. Add the bicarbonate of soda and washing soda and blitz for around 2 minutes until fine.

3. Add the oil and blitz for another minute or two.

4. Store the washing powder in a watertight container.

HOMEMADE WOOL WASH

Woollens need to be treated with care: hand-washed in a good-quality detergent and dried flat. There are many commercial products available, but I like this eucalyptus wool mix, made famous by Martha Gardner. She gave out the recipe freely over the radio over several decades, and many people (including my nana) faithfully copied it out and used it. Most people prefer to buy the commercial version, but once you know how to make it yourself it doesn't take much time and saves a lot of money—it costs around $1.73 a batch.

1 bar pure soap
2 cups boiling water
½ cup methylated spirits
1 tablespoon eucalyptus oil

METHOD:

1. Grate the soap using the grater attachment of a food processor or a box grater.

2. Add the boiling water to the soap flakes and stir to combine. Leave for around 10 minutes, then add the methylated spirits and eucalyptus oil. Transfer to a container to set.

3. To use, dissolve 1 teaspoon of the wool wash in a basin of hot water.

EARLY TO BED — JUST LIKE GRANDMA SAID

In our modern society, we may be rich in terms of possessions. But there is one thing that we are invariably all poor in, and that is sleep.

Our modern lifestyle does not encourage sleep. There are too many distractions that keep us up late — television, mobile phones, Facebook, Instagram, electric lights. I am not suggesting that we go back to the dark ages and dispense with the light, but it is important to understand the effect that all these distractions have on our natural sleep cycle. There are very few people who go to bed with the sunset and get up at dawn. Yet if you think about it, this is probably one of the best things for our bodies and certainly a great way to save on electricity and heating costs! Even going to bed an hour or so earlier would help.

You know what it feels like when you have been up half the night with a sick child or you are nursing a hangover. It's hard to feel positive and resilient or have the energy to do much. I know this intellectually, and I also know that I thrive on a lot of sleep, but I am such a late-night procrastinator. There is always one email I have not read yet, one more thing to do in the kitchen, more clothes to fold up or to hang out, or one more thing to post on Facebook or to comment on. Before I know it, it is already half an hour past when I thought I would start heading to bed. Or an hour.

Does this make me more productive? No, not at all. It means that I am late getting up the next morning, rushed, prone to getting angry and then find it easy to forget things. I also feel tired at work and am less likely to exercise at lunchtime and more likely to indulge in over-sugared tea and chocolate to make me feel better. That then creates a rolling cycle — less exercise and too much sugar makes it harder to get a decent quality of sleep, which then makes me feel even more tired.

So it's not just getting to bed early that helps us sleep better, but having a healthier diet and lifestyle as well. On a recent holiday to visit my mother, she shared that she has given up eating anything sweet at

HOT CHOCOLATE MIX

My kids love hot chocolate with marshmallows. It is a special, occasional winter treat—especially when skiing. However, drinking warm things can also help to keep us feeling warm and reduce our reliance on heating.

Commercial hot chocolate mixes are easy to buy, but they can be very expensive. I am not even going to pretend this is healthy, but at least you know what is in it. I like my mix sweet, but it is easy to reduce the amount of sugar in this recipe or substitute a non-refined sweetener.

2 cups milk powder
1 cup sugar
½ cup coffee whitener
   (you can substitute milk powder, but this helps the mixture dissolve better)
⅓ cup cocoa powder

1. Combine all ingredients in a blender or food processor.

2. Process for around 5 minutes. (The processing time is important to reduce the size of the granules, which makes it easier for the mix to dissolve.) Store in a dry, airtight container for up to a year.

3. To prepare a hot chocolate, dissolve 1 or 2 tablespoons of the mix in a cup of hot water. Top up with milk and add marshmallows, if desired.

COST:
   Milk powder — $1
   Sugar — 15c
   Coffee whitener — 65c
   Cocoa powder — 50c
   Total: $2.30 (about 9c a serve)

least an hour before bed. She said she has noticed she sleeps much, much better when she does this. I was surprised that it would have such a strong effect, but I must admit that in the few days I stayed with her I felt great. We all went to bed super-early, and most days I was up before dawn. And what a beautiful dawn it was, watching the sun rise over the water at Southport on the Gold Coast. Just magic.

The 'early to bed and early to rise' lifestyle is also frugal. Rather than wasting a lot of electricity and gas keeping your home warm and bright late into the night, use solar energy and follow the natural rhythm of the sun where possible. Imagine the savings if you turned off your heating an hour before you usually did. Even if you don't go to sleep that early, consider snuggling into bed with a hot chocolate and a book. It will probably make for a better evening, and you will save energy and money as well.

FRUGALISTA CHALLENGE

Can you reduce your energy bill by 20 per cent compared with the same time last year? Or can you reduce it even further? Decide what changes you'll make to try to achieve your goal. When your next bill arrives, instead of dreading opening it, you'll be excited to see how much you've saved. See how low you can go!

CHAPTER 4

EAT LIKE A QUEEN

Saving on groceries

FEEDING A FAMILY

Growing up, my sister and I spent a lot of time with my Nana Irene. Until I was around ten, she and my grandfather lived on a farm just north of Melbourne. They kept chooks and Nana used the eggs in her cakes. Breakfast was usually hot buttered toast with homemade quince jelly, made from the generous fruit on her tree. The jelly often candied in storage, and I felt an almost guilty pleasure in thinking I was eating lollies on toast.

Most of our meals were on the frugal spectrum. For instance, lunch often featured fried potato latkes, which Nana called 'mock fish', in deference to a time when it was served as a fish substitute. She was a depression-era child, then a war bride, raised children in a Melbourne working-class suburb and fed her family on limited supplies. She was more frugal than I will ever be, but my sister and I didn't once think of Nana's offerings as being cheap or unappetising. On the contrary, we loved eating what she produced in her kitchen—especially her many cakes and slices. Her cooking continues to inspire my food blogging, and now that I am a mother with my own children to feed, I often reflect on my time with Nana in her kitchen. Like hers, my cooking is an extension of my love for my family. The food I produce in my kitchen rarely has anything to do with a price tag. Of course, my kids will nag for processed supermarket junk when it features cartoon characters, and often I will give in. However, just because something costs more doesn't necessarily mean they like it more or that it is more nutritious for them. They will often forget about the packaged food when I present them with a homemade treat fresh out of the oven.

Many cultures have cuisines that stem from financial hardship and the creativity of loving mothers, grandmothers and other cooks. Many such dishes are now modern fare in restaurants and you often pay a premium to eat them, even though they started as rustic meals made from ingredients that were cheap and readily available.

Modern Italian cooking owes many of its influences to *cucina povera* (literally, 'poor cooking') because this was often the food that was cooked at home and remembered so fondly. This style of cooking often uses more seasonal vegetables, less meat and less fatty ingredients than other foods. Examples include pizza (without heavy cheeses or meats), *minestra* (vegetable soup), antipasto (roasted red capsicum and pickled or preserved vegetables), and simple homely meals like *pasta e fagioli* (pasta and beans) and pasta with simple sauces (e.g. *spaghetti aglio e olio*, made from olive oil and garlic).

It's not just true of Italian cooking: any time a community rises out of poverty, it creates a new cuisine born of necessity. Many Singaporean dishes, such as the iconic warming pork bone soup (*bak kut teh*), are believed to have been invented in lean times. Chinese fried rice is best made from leftover rice (in fact, it is not nearly as good made with fresh rice), and congee turns rice from dinner into porridge rice for breakfast.

When I lived in Taiwan, I noticed the revival of dishes that were invented out of necessity when times were tough. This includes 'red cooking' or stewing tofu, egg and offal (a lot tastier than it sounds!), local vegetables such as loofah (*sigua*) and sweet potato leaves (*digua ye*), cumquat sauce accompanying poultry such as goose, slow-cooked pork belly stew (*lu rou fan*) designed to make rice go further, fresh milkfish congee (milkfish is a bony fish that is plentiful and cheap) and whole baked sweet potatoes.

If you haven't guessed by now, I love food and I love cooking. My enjoyment of good food continued — in fact, it was something I rejoiced in — during my $50 a week challenge. I rejoiced in the creativity of living on a lower budget and rose to the challenge.

LIVING ON $50 A WEEK

In August 2016, I stood in front of my pantry and surveyed the bulging mess. Then I opened my fridge, freezer and the cupboards above the fridge where I had even more food stored.

I had to face the fact that I was a hoarder. I had mountains of edible food, even though I had made a conscious effort not to spend much money on groceries for two and a half years. I remembered what it was like to throw out (and donate) lots of food before I left for Taiwan and again when I moved back to Australia, and how sad I felt to waste so much. I started with a clean slate and an empty cupboard, and vowed I would never let that happen again. Yet somehow, I had enough food to survive for months in the unlikely event of a nuclear holocaust. (I would probably have other issues to worry about if this was the case!)

This realisation was the genesis of my $50 a week challenge, which lasted a year. (Coincidentally, Jody Allen's inspirational book *The $50 Weekly Shop* was published around halfway through my own challenge.) While living on a lower food budget requires planning and often more time in food preparation, I managed to live on $50 a week while working full-time and being a mum to two active young boys. Oddly, I found it easier: buying less meant fewer decisions about what to cook, and less time unpacking groceries and later throwing out food that had gone bad.

I was also inspired by several other food and grocery challenges I had completed. From 2014, a year of fiscal restraint, I had tried to reduce my daily food budget from $15 to $12 a day. In 2015, I went down to $10 a day — $70 a week. Things were tight at that time, primarily due to my separation.

In mid-2015, I started blogging as Ms Frugal Ears. The focus initially was on writing '$5 Fridays' posts, where I published meals that cost me $5 or less to make. The previous year I had won a contest run by YWCA Canberra for the best potluck meal under $5. The contest was a fundraiser for emergency food supplies, and encouraged people to host a potluck meal and share recipes that cost only $5 to make.

An issue, I discovered from talking to YWCA, is that many people no longer know how to cook at home with confidence — let alone make low-cost meals. Supermarkets and food producers sponsor most glossy food magazines or food television shows, and they tend to encourage using higher cost ingredients. I was intrigued by this trend and decided I would write regularly about $5 meals.

I'm amazed by the number of people, including some talented food blogger friends, who tell me that it's not possible to cook something for $5 that could be taken to a potluck event. It *can* be done, and I have been doing it for over four years. Many items you'd find on a restaurant menu cost less than $5 to make, but because the techniques are a bit fancy, people don't try them at home. Homemade fettuccine made with eggs from someone's backyard chickens, finished with a sauce made from burnt butter and homegrown sage, for instance, probably costs around $1, even if you lash out and shave some good-quality cheese on top.

Was living on only $50 a week hard? Yes… and no.

For most of the year, I cooked for myself and my two young boys. My boys, who were only four and seven at the time, are fussy eaters and do not eat a lot. They also had dinner with their dad a few nights a week. I did not starve them or deprive them. We still indulged in ice-cream Fridays (our longstanding tradition), cheese streamers for lunches, and treats like Tiny Teddy biscuits and squishy yoghurts, which were not purchased often and so they appreciated them much more.

I supplemented this by baking things like muffins, banana cake and Anzac biscuits for school lunches. I made their favourite meals, such as slow-cooked butter-roasted chicken, risotto (using homemade stock made from the chicken carcass), Taiwanese pudding (a type of crème caramel served in little jars) and Japanese curry (made from scratch). In winter, when it was cold and supplies were running low, my boys would wake to the smell of fresh, warm, super-soft bread from the breadmaker. We kept up our Sunday morning tradition of pancakes in the shape of gingerbread men — made with my own pre-mix or from a simple flour, milk and egg recipe.

When I was cooking just for myself, I didn't need to spend much on food. (A big disclaimer here: I am a short, overweight woman who really shouldn't eat much in the first place! I am also a foodie regularly eating out at events, often for sponsored food review purposes or work functions. Some of these places are a bit swanky and often lead to a bit of overindulging.)

I entertained semi-regularly, following my loaves and fishes approach to entertaining—I figure that whatever I have at home will stretch to feed however many guests I have. I rarely panic about people coming over and race out to buy big cheese platters or expensive wine. I often baked items for work morning teas or church functions, and people often asked me for recipes (even when my offerings were super frugal). I believe generosity comes from the heart, and cooking is an expression of love.

Neil came over for dinner regularly, even before we were dating. I made Japanese chestnut rice and Chinese-style pork hotpot the first time he came over, completing it with bread and butter pudding for dessert. After a while, he started inviting himself over. He put the moves on me while I was in the kitchen making him a lemon and cream pasta alongside a wintery apple, carrot and sesame salad, with a bit of home-made limoncello as a digestif.

The challenge stopped after just over a year. Neil and I started dating in August, and by October he was staying over regularly. He had been stretching my $50 a week budget by bringing over food and treats, used as bribery for my kids. He worked close to a shopping centre, so would often go to ALDI or Costco on the way home from work. Who was I to criticise a man who voluntarily does the grocery shopping, especially when he is good at buying things on special and anticipates what we need?

Over the course of the year, I saved around $100 a week (or $5200) from following the $50 a week challenge. I also reduced food waste and saved time by not buying so many items and then throwing them out at the end of the week. Our overall food budget is now less than $100 a week, which is still lower than the $336 a week that the average two adult and two children family spends (according to the ABS Household Expenditure Survey 2015–16).

Neil had a heart attack in December, just nine days after we announced our engagement (we are pretty sure the two events are not related!). When he came home from hospital, he requested a higher-quality protein than I would normally buy. Having nearly lost him, I wasn't about to deny him a lean piece of steak, pork fillet or some salmon cutlets.

Over time I am slowly influencing Neil about frugal choices, and our shopping habits are changing. He still loves the upper range ALDI muesli for breakfast, for instance, but we now mix it with a cheaper muesli and I serve it with homemade yoghurt, and in winter we often have porridge for breakfast. (Porridge is one of the cheapest items you can cook for breakfast and is also one of the most nutritious.) We enjoy a quality steak on our mini barbecue, but we also enjoy a slow-cooked beef casserole using cheaper gravy steak. We are now conscious of eating more heart-friendly foods in line with Heart Foundation guidelines. I am finding many of these are 'frugal', such as seasonal fruit and vegetables, and legumes. Neil remarked recently that he eats less meat than he did before he met me. He likes chickpeas and we bulk out mince with red kidney beans to make chilli con carne.

MY TOP TEN TIPS

While I no longer do the $50 a week challenge, we still implement many aspects of it. Below are some of the tips I gleaned from the challenge.

1. Reduce food waste

A key reason for doing a $50 a week challenge is to reduce food waste. According to the 2016 RaboDirect Food and Farming Report, on average, most Australians throw away 14 per cent of weekly groceries, amounting to around $1100 per year, while younger people in the Gen Y bracket throw away 20 per cent. This is despite 72 per cent of males and 83 per cent of females surveyed feeling unhappy when food was wasted. The report noted that food wastage was directly linked to personal financial happiness. 'To put it simply, when we take responsibility for our finances through careful budget planning, we waste less, save more and improve our financial wellbeing,' the report concluded.

One day I had a conversation with my sister, Spring, who liked to joke about my frugal ways (along with others in my family). She told me that over Christmas she had spent a few days rearranging her cupboards, as you do when you are having a staycation and looking for things to do.

'I was really inspired by your $50/week challenge,' she said as she showed me her 'before' and 'after' photos of her pantry. 'I think I need to do something similar as I threw out eight grocery bags of food during my cleanout. That's obscene!'

I, too, was shocked. 'Surely you could still use that apple juice?' I suggested, pointing to some plastic bottles of amber-coloured liquid.

'Oh, that's pineapple juice that has gone rancid. I bought it three years ago to make pina coladas but never got around to it.'

That was my pina colada moment, which made me reassess how privileged I was and how important the $50 a week budget was in reducing waste. A generation or so ago in Australia, people would not have bought the ingredients to make cocktails as part of their weekly grocery shopping. Some people can still remember what it was like to have restricted food choices due to post-war rationing. Here was my sister, working in a stressful job, always busy and throwing out bottles of tropical pineapple juice because she didn't have enough time to make cocktails. I could certainly relate as I thought about what my pantry said about me and my priorities.

It isn't just packaged food that many of us waste. Before my $50 a week challenge, I used to buy too much fruit and vegetables and end up throwing out some after a week or two. I would get so excited by the possibilities when I went shopping and think that I would make this, that and the other from the wonderful produce I found.

The main trick to reducing food waste is not to buy too much in the first place. It sounds easy, but look around you at the overflowing trolleys next time you are at the supermarket and you will see how mainstream over-purchasing is. Another key trick is to use up every part of the fruit, vegetable, meat or other items that you have. I use celery tops, for instance, rather than throw them out. Neil likes to eat a whole carrot with the skin on. Leftover carrot pulp from making fresh juice becomes a carrot cake. Apple skins and cores can be used to make apple cider vinegar or apple jelly. Lemon rind is perfect for making limoncello, grating into cake batters or cleaning bathrooms. The ends of cucumbers are a refreshing face tonic on a hot day, and cold tea bags make great compresses for tired eyes. Soggy lettuce is perfect for feeding backyard chickens. Meat offcuts can be made into soup or given as a treat to a neighbour's dog.

2. Make an inventory

The first step to doing a $50 a week challenge is to start using up what you have. To do this, I found it helpful to examine what I had and make an inventory. A key to cutting back your grocery bill is recognising that you probably already have a lot of food. When you are conscious of it, you will see that abundance is everywhere and for most middle-class Australians at least, you are not going to starve. Of course, many people *are* starving in the world and there are people experiencing serious poverty in Australia, which is all the more reason to be grateful for what you have and ensure you don't waste it. If you're reading this book and you are struggling, make sure you get in touch with one of the many charities that has a food bank program.

I am a busy working mother with kids and a writing addiction (read: 'housework is not my priority'). Ideally, to do this step thoroughly you would take out all the food from your fridge and pantry, rearrange it nicely and do up an itemised spreadsheet that includes the full cost of all items. You could even put things into nice containers. If you plan to spring clean anyway, you might find this liberating. I do not have the energy to do this. Instead, when I make an inventory, I clean out one shelf in my pantry at a time. I remove all the food and wipe the shelf. Then I write a list of what is in there, make an estimate of the costs and put it neatly back in. I find it helps to put the list of food on the pantry door. I then make a conscious effort to use up what is on that shelf.

When I did this before the challenge, I did a rough estimate of the value of the food sitting on one of my pantry shelves (see over).

Maria biscuits (ALDI)	$0.80
Cake decorating set	$10.00
Dried fungus (new)	$2.30
Black fungus, dried (quarter of a packet)	$0.50
Pasta bows	$0.50
Macaroni	$0.70
Soup pasta	$0.40
Lasagne sheets (ALDI)	$1.50
Dried bonito flakes	$0.50
Couscous (wholemeal)	$1.00
Campbell's Country Ladle soup	$1.50
Desiccated coconut	$1.50
Currants (half a packet)	$1.00
Arborio rice (ALDI)	$2.49
Leggo's pizza sauce	$2.00
Jatz biscuits	$2.00
Taiwanese brown sugar	$1.00
Caramel pour (ALDI — bought in error)	$1.80

Dried feverfew flowers (from the garden)	$0.00
Home-roasted peanuts	$0.50
Indian snacks	$0.50
Ramen noodles	$0.80
Vermicelli noodles	$0.50
Passionfruit pulp	$1.00
Pialligo Estate plum jam	$6.00
5 gourmet sauces/jams (gifted by Neil's friend)	$36.00
Cranberries (half a packet)	$0.70
Peanut butter (three half-empty jars)	$4.00
Vegemite (one nearly full jar)	$5.00
Liquid glucose	$2.00
Japanese seaweed sprinkles (for making rice rolls)	$1.00
Canned tuna (ALDI)	$1.80
2 packets Oats Sensations	$0.40
Honey (three half-empty jars)	$2.00
Very old apple sauce	$0.30
	$93.99

Once I added it up, I realised that one shelf of food alone was worth nearly $100. That's two weeks' worth of grocery money right there! And I have five shelves in my pantry (and more food in other cupboards). You might tell yourself that the excess food in your pantry is there in case of an emergency. How often do we experience a famine in our modern cities? More likely you will have to throw most of it out when it goes off. It is far better to stop overbuying now and use up the food you have in creative ways.

Doing an inventory is like preparing for a garage sale: by decluttering and reorganising, you realise how much you have and how much you don't need. It helps you to make better decisions when you are in the supermarket as you know what you already have and that you are well prepared for potential contingencies.

3. Write a meal plan

You are far more likely to only buy what you need if you have confidence that you have enough ingredients at home for key meals. You don't have to be super-organised to prepare a meal plan. Simply sitting down over a cup of tea or coffee and mapping out what you are going to eat for the week ahead will save you hours. The last thing I want to be doing is queuing up during the 6 pm rush at the supermarket buying ingredients for dinner. Yes, that was me when I first moved to Canberra. However, I got better with time.

Many years ago, when we hosted homestay students, I used to meal plan religiously. I was responsible for preparing three meals a day for our students, so I needed to know what I was going to cook for the week. If you have a big family, or if you are eating on a tight budget, meal planning becomes even more important.

I now have an organised yet flexible approach to meal planning. I like to first identify nights when I might be eating out. I then write down meals for the remaining nights. In my meal planning matrix, I also include ideas for other meals (sometimes I change my mind because I feel like cooking something else). I also include a list of food items that I want to use up that week so that I know what to focus on.

Below is an example of a meal plan of actual meals that I ate during my $50 a week challenge.

Sunday night: Rice, broccolini, pork, tofu and sweet corn stir-fry; pickled watermelon rind; watermelon. I baked a batch of banana, Weet-Bix and choc-chip muffins for the kids.

Monday: Sardine pizza, zucchini slice and blackberry shrub. (The kids have been really into sardine pizza since they read in a Golden Book that it was Donald Duck's favourite.)

Tuesday: Leftover zucchini slice for lunch; homemade kimchi dumplings (*jiaozi*) from the freezer for dinner. The kids had dinner with their dad.

Wednesday: Brown rice, leftover pork stir-fry and pickled watermelon rind for lunch. Instant noodles and broccolini for my boys (who promptly picked out the broccolini), and pasta with Sichuan sesame sauce and cucumber for me. I had a dessert of steamed pears with rock sugar to help a lingering cough and experimented with making white wine vinegar.

Thursday: Rice with Taiwanese braised pork (*lu rou fan*), stewed egg and broccolini. Watermelon for dessert.

Friday: Leftover *lu rou fan* and rice for lunch. I was unwell in the afternoon and went home early (missing a swanky work function) and ended up eating white toast with Vegemite. The kids were with their dad for dinner.

Saturday: White rice congee and pickled vegetables for breakfast. This is my go-to food when my stomach is unsettled—I find that eating fermented foods really helps. We had various lunch snacks before and after swimming, including at a cafe (oh, what a decadent treat!). In the afternoon we visited a Taiwanese friend, and we feasted on homemade potsticker dumplings, Taiwanese pork belly (*gua bao*), lemon meringue pie and chocolate cake.

4. Always use a shopping list

It might sound obvious that you save money when you make and use a shopping list. Who hasn't gone into the supermarket to buy a loaf of bread and a bottle of milk and come out forgetting to buy the milk? This is not coincidental—supermarkets are retail spaces that are designed to entice you in and encourage impulse buying. Have you ever noticed where the refrigerators housing the milk are? They are not near the entrance, nor near the checkouts. You need to go through the store to get to the milk, which is always located towards the back, thus making it easy to be sidetracked and buy more.

I always have a shopping list on the fridge or on the kitchen bench. Whenever I run out of something, or have nearly run out of something, I write it down. I also add the ingredients that I will need for cooking that week, based on my meal plan. I then take the list with me when I go shopping.

I have tried using grocery shopping apps on my phone, or even 'to do' list functions. The problem I found was that as soon as I looked at my phone, I started checking messages, then Facebook, then email—and before I knew it, I had forgotten to write down anything on my shopping list and my dinner was burning. Perhaps you have better self-discipline than me.

Some people find that shopping online helps reduce impulse buying. I have tried online shopping once or twice, and I found that it didn't work for me. I was cranky because one of the main items I wanted for that week (a whole chicken for slow roasting) was unavailable. I also found that it was more expensive because I couldn't shop at discount supermarkets, like ALDI and Costco.

That said, there are some real benefits to online shopping. It reduces impulse buying by forcing you to focus more critically on your list. You can see how your cart is adding up, so there are no surprises when you get to the checkout. It saves time, which can be valuable if you have something more profitable to do, such as a side hustle like writing a book, for instance. If you live in an inner urban area or somewhere where you could work from home or there are public transport issues, it could mean that you can ditch your car and save between $3000 and $5000 per year.

5. Have a cash kitty

I find I spend less when I spend cash than when I use a debit or credit card. It's so easy to 'tap and go' your fantastic plastic, and you have what you need without even thinking about how much you're spending.

The $50 a week challenge included food, essential toiletries and cleaning products. It also included bottles of wine. I kept the cash in a separate kitty, and I dug into the surplus on occasion (you just can't live without toilet paper!). For example, if I underspent by $17.30 one week, I would add that to my kitty. If I underspent by $20 the next week, I would also add that to my kitty, making a total of $37.30. In the third week I would add my $50 for the week and I would have $87.30 to spend.

6. Buy less meat (and cheaper cuts of meat)

For ten years I was a vegetarian. I wasn't a strict vegetarian—I ate fish and sometimes even chicken. Nonetheless, I liked following a vegetarian diet. I also made sure that I ate vegetarian food on the first and the fifteenth day of the lunar calendar, a practice popular with many Buddhists in Taiwan and other places in Southeast Asia.

The environmental benefits of eating a vegetarian diet are well documented. There is even a 'meat-free Monday' movement that aims to promote vegetarianism one day a week. I no longer follow a vegetarian diet, but I do make a conscious effort to eat less meat. When I do eat meat, I am careful to use up as much of it as possible. We are all part of the cycle of life—an animal gave up its life, and I feel upset if I waste that gift by throwing any of it out.

I believe many of us in Western countries eat too much meat. When I lived in Taiwan, people would buy 150 grams, or maybe 200 grams, of minced pork. Beef was more expensive. However, it now seems normal to buy 2 kilograms or more of mince at a time and to have a large piece of steak or chicken for dinner every night.

Eating less meat can save you money and, if you include more vegetables and legumes, it can be healthier for you as well. Does this sound boring? I find meals based on seasonal fruit and vegetables to be tasty, colourful, flavoursome and engaging. I do, however, understand that not everyone feels quite as excited. My approach is to add more vegetables and legumes into my diet to pad out the meat and make it stretch. For instance, if I am making a bolognese sauce I will add red lentils to make it go further. They hide in the sauce and usually my kids don't notice. Sometimes I might even be able to sneak in some carrot purée or even some shredded zucchini. Rather than eat a whole steak, I will often stir-fry beef strips with vegetables. Or I will slow cook meat with something creative. Lamb chops, for instance, taste delicious when cooked with wine and pearl barley.

I also use cuts of meat that are cheaper. Tougher cuts of red meat are delicious if slow cooked or marinated. I find that they have more flavour and lend themselves well to casseroles and stews. The key is to have patience and understand how to prepare them.

I am also a big fan of chicken drumsticks and chicken wings. Drumsticks sell at ALDI for $5.98 for 2 kilograms. In Chinese kitchens, chicken drumsticks (and in fact any meat close to the bone) are prized. There is a surprising amount of flesh on a chicken drumstick. They are delicious baked, casseroled or barbecued, or you can cut the flesh away from the bone and use it for meals like stir-fries. Make sure you keep the bones as they are fantastic for making stock.

I once had a young homestay student from China who loved chicken wings. They are expensive to buy in China, yet incredibly cheap in Australia. I like to bake them with homemade plum sauce and sesame seeds, or marinate them in a five-spice powder, brown sugar and sesame oil mixture and fry them. You can even stew them in Coca-Cola (seriously, this is good, and since I don't drink soft drinks it's a great way to use up flat leftovers). Chicken wings are a party favourite, and many people don't realise how cheap they are. I've been to many shindigs where people demolish spicy chicken wings from Costco.

While some celebrity chefs are on the record saying that they don't do offal, I don't mind a bit occasionally. In Taiwan, it's hard to avoid offal as it's everywhere—and awfully good at times. The trick is to prepare it properly as most types of offal need to be soaked or cleaned before being cooked. Including some offal could be a good way to ensure you have enough minerals in your diet if you are on a low income and can't afford much meat. If you find liver confronting, perhaps start with some gourmet options such as pâté, pasta with sage and chicken liver, roasted or stewed pig's trotters, or Neil's favourite, steak and kidney pie. I'm predicting an offal renaissance, so get in while it's still cheap.

As Neil is recovering from a heart attack and he has a family history of heart disease, we will be going easy on steak and kidney pie or calf liver fry-ups. I also have a family history of high cholesterol, so can only enjoy offal in moderation.

7. Choose your supermarket carefully

Where you shop is almost as important as what you buy. You can buy the same item at one store for a fraction of the price that you would pay at another store.

So, which supermarket? The answer to this question varies depending on a lot of factors including where you live, where you like to shop and the type of food you like to eat. In our household, we are a huge fan of the German supermarket chain ALDI. But if you need to drive an hour out of your way to get to an ALDI store, you might find it easier and more economical to shop elsewhere.

In my first marriage, we ate a lot of Asian food. Much of it was Taiwanese influenced, and it was hard to get ingredients in Canberra. We tended to shop at a select few Asian supermarkets that stocked the brands and products that we liked and topped up on other items when we visited family in Brisbane. There are a lot of Taiwanese migrants in Brisbane, so there were more stores there that sold Taiwanese food and ingredients.

I found in general that prices at Asian supermarkets tend to be lower and the produce (especially fresh fruit and vegetables) tends to be better quality. It depends on what is on special and what you like to eat. Neil, my Queanbeyan-born man, doesn't mind trying Asian food, but he much prefers English- or Australian-style cooking, so I no longer shop at Asian supermarkets as often. That said, I still do shop at Asian supermarkets from time to time and enjoy their low prices. Most stores are family run and situated outside of major shopping centres. As their rental and labour costs are generally lower, they can pass this onto consumers. One of my favourite stores, run by a Vietnamese couple, also supplies many restaurants in Canberra and is essentially a wholesaler. I discovered, somewhat surprisingly, that items like bulk bicarbonate of soda, sesame oil, bags of peanuts, soybeans, spices and certain legumes are much cheaper purchased there.

For spices and most legumes, the best places to shop are Indian or Middle Eastern supermarkets. From time to time I enjoy shopping at a quirky Indian superstore hidden in an industrial suburb in Canberra. From there I buy giant bags of chickpeas (I love how they grade different-sized chickpeas into different bags), lentils, red kidney beans, curry powders, spices, chai tea, henna to dye my hair and make-up such as kohl eyeliner. I find the offerings here much cheaper, and more exciting, than the tiny plastic bags of soup legumes hidden in supermarket aisles.

Canberra has a surprisingly large Costco outlet. On weekends, it is often the social place to be—we nearly always run into someone we know. My kids love coming along because there are usually food samples being handed out. They are, like their mother, fond of 'free food'. I have had to teach them not to yell 'Look, there's free food!', and instead try to refer to the giveaways as 'samples'. The sample items usually seem to end up in our shopping trolley, thanks to the nag factor of the kids.

Our favourite Costco items are meat (rotisserie roast chickens, minced beef, pork steaks), hard cheeses for pasta, bulk Devondale butter, flour for baking, bread, clothing, petrol, nappies (when my kids were little) and toilet paper (their biggest seller nationally). Costco is a good place to go to stock up for a party: their alcohol is cheap and good value, and they do large sandwich platters, salad boxes and super-large pizzas.

A Costco membership costs $60 a year, so you need to shop there regularly for the cost to be worthwhile. However, one little-known advantage to Costco shopping is that if you buy an electronic product or similar, Costco will refund or replace it if it breaks, as long as you keep your membership current. So, if you buy a vacuum cleaner and four years later it stops working, Costco will refund or replace it—no need for you to purchase additional insurance.

For me, the big disincentive of shopping at Costco is the sheer size of everything. Even as a family, I often feel like there is no way known I could get through everything in my bulk purchases. We usually complete our shopping expedition with an ice-cream for the kids or a $1.99 hot dog with a bottomless cup of soft drink. As I sit and contemplate the enormity of everything—the food, our purchases, the store itself—I can't help but wonder what I'm doing here. That said, the feeling soon dissipates when I think about the bargains I have found.

We do most of our weekly shopping at ALDI. Their seven-day deals, especially the fruit and vegetables, are hard to match anywhere else. I find several of the food items are as good or better than Costco. And if you want to buy something like flour, you only need to buy 1 kilogram rather than 10 kilograms. I don't have the space at home to shop wholesale all the time, so ALDI is the place we go to shop for our day-to-day items.

The trap with ALDI shopping is that it's so easy to overspend on their Special Buys. Just this week we came away with two pairs of hiking shoes, a green pullover and two toys—none of which were on my shopping list. My good friend, Trish, deliberately avoids shopping in any of the middle aisles at ALDI to prevent impulse purchases.

For many years the market in Australia has been dominated by two main players: Woolworths and Coles. My dad insists on shopping at Woolworths because he likes the range and the fact that they offer a full service, so he only needs to go to one store. They have a delicatessen, a large range of fruit and vegetables, and more cleaning items than you would ever possibly need. I shop at Woolworths or Coles for niche items that I can't buy at ALDI, including unusual pasta shapes, aspirin, light bulbs, pure soap and lectic soda (which I use for homemade washing powder—see page 74).

If you prefer shopping at Woolworths or Coles over ALDI or Costco, you are not necessarily paying a higher price on every item. When Neil and I did a $2 a day challenge recently, we were surprised to find that Woolworths was on par—and in some cases cheaper—than ALDI on some items.

The emergence of quality home-brand products such as the Woolworths Select range is also ensuring that good-quality items are available at lower prices to consumers. Some Select products have won awards, which testifies to their quality. However, in general, I find that when I compare a basket of similar or identical groceries, Costco is the cheapest, followed by ALDI, Woolworths and Coles.

8. Ditch the shopping trolley

A shopping trolley is one of the biggest disruptions that hit the grocery market last century. The humble basket on wheels took a while to take off, but when it did it made inventor Sylvan Goldman a fortune.

Using a shopping trolley is dangerous for the frugalista. It's so easy to lose perspective about how much you have purchased because you don't have to physically carry it (at least not until you get home—more on that later).

Years ago, I worked with someone who worked hard and had a good job. My friend earned much more than the average salary in Australia. However, he threw it all in to go and work for the family shopping trolley repair business. It seemed odd for a university-educated professional to go and fix trolleys for a living. However, he told me that it was a lucrative business as supermarkets will pay a fortune to fix trolleys. They know that a broken trolley—such as one that has a wonky wheel that makes it difficult to push around—can cause thousands of dollars in lost sales. Supermarkets want you to use nice big trolleys that wheel around easily so that you can spend up big. When you have the convenience of a trolley, it is so easy to keep walking around a supermarket, and the empty trolley almost begs you to fill it up.

Some supermarkets have attached GPS trackers to monitor the movement of trolleys around their stores. Often this research shows how much people (usually women) dillydally—consumers rarely rush in and rush out, but spend time hunting and gathering through the aisles. The best way to avoid idling (and spending) in the supermarket is to carry what you buy, so you get a sense of how much you are buying.

For years I did two shops a week—one on Saturday, when I would leave my boys with their dad. I'd fill up a backpack or plastic bags with groceries and walk home, 20 to 30 minutes uphill. That alone made me assess whether what looked appealing was a need or a want. I then did a second shop mid-week, when picking up my boys.

I love grocery shopping—the excitement of finding new products, of discovering seasonal fruit and vegetables on sale, and selecting lots of delicious food to enjoy later. If I use a trolley, I usually fill it up. However, that sense of retail joy quickly vanishes after I pay and get things back to the car. Once I get everything home, I then have the job of carrying not one, but three bags of shopping upstairs from the underground carpark to my apartment. I am doing this while kid-wrangling and then have to find places for my purchases in the fridge, freezer and pantry. It is easier when Neil is with me, but even so, it can take hours to sort through everything—rolled oats into the dispenser, ice-cream in the freezer, vegetables into the crisper, finding inventive places to store items because we have too much.

Unless you need to do a large shop, try to ditch the trolley next time you are out shopping, and see what a difference it makes. I suspect that not only will you buy less, but you will be more focused on ensuring you pick up the items on your list that you actually need.

9. Try urban foraging

Imagine you are in Tuscany or Eastern Europe. Imagine you are on a food tour high in the mountains, searching for truffles, rare berries, nuts and unusual herbs. Now stop and consider what you might be able to find in your own neighbourhood. You can find some amazing food growing for free. Even on the walk to drop my kids off to school I usually come home with a few wild borage flowers, olives or edible weeds.

Not long after I started blogging about frugal food, I decorated a risotto dish with fresh dandelion flowers. After someone told me that no-one would be interested in eating weeds, I became determined to find out more, and curiosity led me to look at the environment around me in a new way. I was struggling to find time to plant my vegetable patch, so I decided I might as well start by using what was growing wild in my garden. I have been blessed to learn so much from my blogging friend Susan Hutchinson from Susan's Sumptuous Suppers, who regularly leads edible weed tours through Canberra's Environment Centre.

I believe in urban foraging not because I am destitute, but because it is local and sustainable. You don't need to use fertilisers or pesticides to grow wild food, and often the food would be killed with chemicals if it wasn't harvested and eaten. Nor do you need to travel far as it is generally available locally. Urban foraging also connects you with the seasons. I find I am more attuned to seasonal changes and notice when it is best to harvest. Many lettuce-like weeds are at their best in early spring, especially when there is enough rain. For instance, I fashioned a simple chicken salad using a mixture of homegrown lettuce, rocket and garden weeds, with a dressing made from lemons that I had been given. All the greenery was sourced from my garden when I still lived in a suburban house, and I tossed in whatever was in my fridge that I wanted to use up.

At first, I was terrified that I would eat something poisonous—some people have died agonising deaths in Canberra from eating death cap mushrooms. It's criticial to seek expert advice before eating any wild mushrooms. However, once you know how to spot edible weeds, you're unlikely to mistakenly eat anything harmful. Most weeds growing in your garden or neighbourhood are probably safe in any case, or you will know about them if they are not, but you should still do your own careful research. And unless you have sprayed weed killer on edible weeds, they are unlikely to be toxic. Nonetheless, if you're ever in doubt about the safety of any wild foods, it's best to leave them alone.

One of my favourite resources is the public Facebook group 'Edible weeds, wild food & foraging in Australia'. You can post pictures of plants you find that you might want to eat but are unsure of, and also observe what other people are finding and eating.

Below are some of the foods that I forage for in my neighbourhood.

- **Blackberries:** Blackberries are high in antioxidants, good for the heart and a natural aphrodisiac. Young leaves can be made into tea and are good for lactating mothers. Berries are ripe in January and February. Blackberries are a noxious weed in Canberra and surrounding areas and thus plentiful. You will know if they have been sprayed as the chemicals are tinted pink and there will be warning signs posted.

- **Dandelions:** The leaves of the dandelion plant have strong medicinal properties, including as a liver tonic. Eat them in early spring to help detox your system. Yes, the leaves are bitter—I like to stir-fry them with garlic and oyster sauce, which helps to mask the bitter taste. Flowers are edible and pretty in a salad. The roots can be dug up, roasted and used as a highly diuretic coffee substitute. It takes a bit of effort to get the dirt off and I have not had the perseverance, but if you are trying to move away from coffee, this could be worth trying.

- **Purslane:** Purslane flourishes in many home gardens over summer. It has the highest concentration of Omega 3 of any land-based plant, and is good for reducing heart disease and the risk of stroke. Dr Oz (who has appeared on *The Oprah Winfrey Show*) has declared purslane to be an essential 'superfood' and claims it is a secret beauty food, due to its anti-ageing properties. You can eat it raw in a salad or add it to a curry or stew.

- **Fennel:** Fennel grows wild by roadsides in many parts of Australia. The fronds and seeds are good for digestion. Fennel tea has aphrodisiac properties for women, and it is good for women experiencing menstruation and menopause, and lactating mothers. I like to pick fronds in early spring and make them into a fennel aperitif liqueur. I also drink it as a tea and use it in pasta dishes and omelettes. It has a similar taste to aniseed and dill.

- **Plums:** Many prunus trees were planted in Canberra for their beautiful spring blossoms. In early summer, they fruit, producing small plums that look like cherries but taste sour and not as appetising as cherries. However, they make the most marvellous jam with a depth and tartness that is hard to match with commercial plums. At lunchtimes, I can often be found near my work picking plums to bring back home to make into Christmas gifts.

- **Rosehips:** Rosehips are rich in vitamin C and are harvested around the same time that many people need a bit of a vitamin C burst to help their bodies fight off colds and flus. They can be dried and made into a tea or simmered with sugar and water to make a cordial. They can also be combined with a carrier oil such as almond or olive to make a rich oil for the skin. A word of warning: rosehips also have strong laxative qualities. Consume them in moderation.

- **Rosemary:** Rosemary grows so well where I live in Canberra that it almost goes wild in some places, and I've been known to snip off a bit as I walk past a hedge to use in cooking. It's delicious roasted with potatoes and other root vegetables. I love sprinkling it on potato pizzas in early spring, when it is flowering. I also like to dry rosemary and lightly pulverise it with salt, which I then sprinkle on chicken drumsticks and potato wedges before baking them.

- **Olives:** Olive trees are often planted as ornamental trees, and in some places they have virtually gone wild. The fruit is edible, but it takes time to brine it. I have been brining my own olives for a few years now. It takes time and patience, but the result is tasty homemade olives produced without any preservatives. They taste quite different to store-bought ones.

- **Mint:** Mint grows prolifically in damp, shady conditions. It has spread to some waterways, where it grows happily beside creeks and rivers. Mint can be used in cooking—think Vietnamese spring rolls and soups—or made into mint juleps to drink. You can also make it into a tea. Mint replants and regenerates easily, so if you find some growing nearby, chances are you can take it home and replant it.

- **Hawthorn:** Early English settlers extensively grew hawthorn trees to help fence in stock, and they are now the bane of many farmers. Hawthorn is especially prolific in some areas of New South Wales, almost to the point of being noxious. Hawthorn leaves can be made into a subtle, sweet tea. Hawthorn berries can be used for jams and jellies or made into a tincture with brandy. Hawthorn has been traditionally used for heart conditions and is also reputed to be an aphrodisiac.

- **Cleavers:** In early spring, many home gardens fill up with these fast-growing weeds that, somewhat annoyingly, cling to you if you brush past them. I used to spend hours weeding them out, then I discovered that they are high in antioxidants, especially when juiced. I think of them like wheat grass, but free and readily available. They are perfect for an early spring detox.

- **Apples:** Many country areas in south-eastern Australia have apple trees growing wild on the roadside. I don't know how they got there, but I'm guessing it was via the car window. They now produce tasty apples in autumn and most have not been sprayed. They don't look pretty like store-bought apples, however they cook up well into apple pie or apple sauce.

10. Reduce the alcohol

In many Australian households, we probably do not think of wine or other alcohol as part of our weekly grocery budget. It has become something we drink to relax at the end of a difficult day or week.

Have you ever stopped and added up how much you spend on what you drink? That bottle of wine might only cost $10, but if you are consuming one a night (presumably not on your own), that's $70 a week right there. That's not counting how much you might spend going out, or dining with friends and so on.

A friend of mine, who I did not pick as being a heavy drinker, gave up alcohol for a year. She estimated she saved between $2000 and $3000 in that year. Think about how often and how much you drink when you go out, and what you could save if you gave up, reduced or even halved the amount that you drink.

According to the Foundation for Alcohol Research and Education (FARE), the average Australian household spends $32.20 per week on alcohol ($1674.40 per year), which makes up 1.9 per cent of their total weekly household expenditure. Note that this is average—given that many people do not drink for religious or other reasons, the other households are probably making up for more than their fair share.

I have not battled alcohol addiction, but I know several people who have. I find alcohol is scarily pervasive in Australian culture, and I find there are many social situations where there is pressure to drink. I noticed this especially when I returned to Australia after having lived in Taiwan for three and a half years. Yes, people drink there, and you can buy beer, wine and even spirits at convenience stores everywhere, but most people don't tend to go crazy with alcohol.

Neither Neil nor I are big drinkers, and we can happily go without alcohol. At one stage I considered giving it up entirely. We tend to have a glass or two on a Friday night when we are singing karaoke, and maybe a glass with dinner on a Saturday or Sunday. That's it—we save our alcohol consumption for weekends and events. We also enjoy quality lower-priced wines. And we reduced costs at our wedding by serving homemade beer, ginger beer, apple cider, lemonade and punch.

FRUGALISTA CHALLENGE

Try to reduce your grocery expenditure to $25 per family member for a week. For example, $100 for a family of four. Start by taking an inventory of your pantry and fridge. Based on what you find, write a meal plan for the week, then write a shopping list. Put the cash in your purse and use that, and only that, for all your grocery spending for the week. If you find it's not too hard, then keep going for a second week.

CHAPTER 5

THE FRUGAL FASHIONISTA

Saving on clothes

DRESSING LIKE AN EMPRESS

Neil and I stood in front of DIVA, Home of Diamonds museum in the old town of Antwerp in Belgium. Neil was dressed in an Australian-made black tuxedo. I was also sporting Australian design in a slimming black and silver Anthea Crawford formal dress. A friend on the delegation insisted on taking a photo, and we looked like a dapper couple, if I do say so myself. We joked later that Neil looked like James Bond (as played by Sean Connery), not in his usual back-of-Queanbeyan country attire of flannelette shirt, jeans and work boots.

We moved on from that event, by police escort, to a gala ball. As we mingled with elegantly dressed Antwerp ladies and chatted with diplomats, diamond experts and diamond traders from around the world, I felt fashionable and even glamourous—like the woman in Peter Sarstedt's classic ballad 'Where Do You Go To My Lovely'.

While I am too short and full-figured to be mistaken for a fashion model, I knew that I looked the part and fitted in. This was no small thing as Antwerp has a reputation of being a style and fashion mecca for the discerning.

Neil's tux cost $25 at an op shop. My dress cost $15. Style has little to do with a price tag. You can look amazing without spending a lot of money. Or you can look like a joke by slavishly following brands.

I used to love the '90s sitcom *Absolutely Fabulous*. In one scene, Edina is struggling with what to wear, in part because she has put on weight. She puts on a garish orange tight-fitting top and pants that are unflattering to her figure and made worse by her over the top heart-shaped jewellery. When her daughter queries her outfit, Edina says, 'It's Lacroix, sweetie, Lacroix … it's a bit tight, isn't it, it's a bit tight, but it's all right maybe, isn't it? People will think, wow, it's Lacroix!' and insists on wearing it. It is one of the funniest television scenes I have ever seen.

How often do you see people who, in a vain attempt to look fashionable, spend a fortune yet end up looking like a fashion tragic? The sad thing is that they have probably spent so much money because they wanted people to know they had style, yet the result is anything but stylish.

You can look gorgeous, fabulous and wonderful without spending a lot of money. You can even do this by wearing clothes that are free. You need not feel like a frumpy second-hand rose just because you haven't spent a lot on fashion.

You can be a stylish frugalista by following my tips on styling and how to get cheap (and even free) fashion. I'll also tell you how I fared in the challenge I gave myself to go without buying any new clothes for a whole year.

MY MOTHER THE FASHION DESIGNER

I am the black sheep of the family. I ended up with a steady public service job. However, I grew up in a rag trade family. When I told my mother, Lee Bird, I was going to write about having a frugal wardrobe, she was not enthusiastic. 'I don't do frugal,' she said. 'That sounds so boring. But I am all about looking fabulous on less.'

Looking fabulous is something Mum knows a lot about. She was a fashion icon in Queensland in the 1980s and 1990s, before 'retiring' to the Gold Coast and operating a fashion boutique in the upmarket Tedder Avenue on Main Beach. These days she prefers to dress in simple black and white, adopting a very Gold Coast casual resort look. When I was growing up in Melbourne, she was into '70s disco, and a decade or so ago everything was matching leopard-skin print.

In the early 1970s, Mum went to London to work. When she returned, she opened a boutique, became pregnant and came up with more designs to sell. She often tells a story about how she once caught a lady shoplifting in the boutique and, while heavily pregnant, chased her down the street and got the dress back. She was a determined woman.

Mum would often do work from home, making patterns and cutting fabric for samples. I would sit under her large industrial cutting table and play with sequins or buttons. I had lots of fun threading lace and ribbons through the holes in the metal edge of the table.

Mum left all of that to make a sea change to Queensland, moving to Noosa and setting up a boutique in Hastings Street in the early '80s. I remember her sewing her early designs—resort dresses fringed with seashells she picked up on the beach—from our garage. She said that she had to train staff from scratch, as there was no fashion industry in Noosa at that time. She built her factory in an industrial area away from the resort town. Eventually, her solo business spread to four boutiques and a national wholesale business. She even sold overseas for a while, with one bright hand-knitted mohair coat being worn by Dolly Parton.

I had a few unsuccessful attempts at learning to sew. For years, I thought that I lacked the fashionista touch that my mum had, in part because I was always frugal and liked op shop clothes. However, I must have absorbed more than I realised by following style tips I learnt while growing up. I might not look like a supermodel (funnily enough, there are only a handful of people in the world who do), but people often comment on what I wear and how I look. I usually have the confidence to feel good in what I wear.

Here are a few tips about style that I picked up from my mum:

1. **Never slavishly follow fashion.** Just because everyone is wearing leg warmers, bell-bottom pants or gingham check, it doesn't mean you should, too. Be guided by what suits you, your shape and your style. If something doesn't look good on you, don't wear it. (To this I would add that despite what the media will have us believe, there is no perfect shape. I am envious of slim, tall and sporty friends; some of them are envious of my substantial cleavage and soft, straight hair. Be proud of who you are and dress according to what looks good on you.)

2. **Do not wear everything in the latest 'in' colour.** Millennial pink, rose gold, lime green or teal blue/green may be the latest 'it' colour, but that doesn't mean everything in your wardrobe should be that colour. You could invest in one jacket, shirt or scarf if you want to get that season's look. That way, when the latest 'in' colour is 'out', you aren't stuck with several outfits that you need to replace.

3. **Black and white works.** Black and white is a classic combination, and it always works well.

4. **Do not wear something unless it looks fabulous on you.** Maybe you think something has potential, that it's a bit interesting but not quite

right. If you are in a change room and you do not feel entirely fabulous and glamorous when you put something on, then just do not go there. If you don't love it then and there, you never will, and it will just clutter your wardrobe. Several times I have been shopping with Mum and come across an item that was a bit 'school girl understated 1960s interesting', with potential but a little drab in a cool way, and wondered if I could pull it off because I like quirky things. 'No way,' my mum would say. 'You can do better.' She was right; I could, and I did.

5. **Keep it simple.** Classic is always in style. Simple, well-made and elegant pieces are an investment. I still have a brown wool suit that I had made in Hoi An, Vietnam, in 2007 that I wear nearly every week. The cut is classic, the materials are quality and it always looks good.

6. **An elegant scarf is an asset.** According to my mother, you cannot have enough scarves: 'Classic basics will never date—by adding a new scarf you create a new outfit.' There are YouTube tutorials on how to tie scarves, but it depends largely on the shape of the scarf and what you are wearing. You don't need an expensive Hermes scarf, just something interesting.

7. **Get rid of anything you haven't worn recently.** Go and have a look in your wardrobe. What items have you thought about wearing in the last four weeks but dismissed? Why? Why didn't you feel good about them? If you keep bypassing certain outfits, there will be a reason. Give them to a friend or a charity shop—they are just taking up valuable space.

8. **Wear clothes that fit you well.** It is often worth the small cost of having quality basic pieces altered. For example, you could have shoulder pads removed, or a coat made smaller or larger. Since I am

short, I often pay to have items taken up at the shoulder so that they are not so low in the body (read: showing lots of cleavage).

9. **Wear your clothes with attitude.** So much of fashion is not about what you wear, but how you project confidence when you're wearing it. Wear something like it is the latest fashion and people will believe that it is. Your dress might be a cheap op shop find, but wear it like it's Chanel and believe in your own style, and you will project yourself as a fashionista.

10. **Smile, smile, smile.** Just like in the song from the musical *Annie*, 'you're never fully dressed without a smile'. No matter what the price tag of your clothes is, nothing can beat a smile. Positivity and laughter are much more attractive to be around than someone who is dour, yet fashionable.

THE $50 BUDGET

For over a decade, my clothes budget has been $50 a month. Only $50 a month? When you consider that many items in boutiques cost double that, it seems like a stretch to survive for a whole month on $50. However, over a year this is $600. When you follow the tips in this chapter, $600 goes a long way.

I don't look shabby on my $50 a month. In my professional career, it's important that I look the part, especially when I am networking or making presentations. I might be giving a presentation or chairing a meeting where each word is interpreted into multiple languages, or maybe responsible for taking notes during important deliberations. Whenever I am in a meeting, I know that I'm dressed fashionably and appropriately.

Next time you are in a meeting, have a look at how people, especially women, are dressed. What are the things you notice? What looks good and what doesn't? If you're not in a job that involves formal meetings, you can observe people walking around a central business district at lunchtime, or even by watching television. In the 1980s it was all about big hair and big shoulder pads. Then, for a while, it was the perfectly tailored suit. More recently I find that a stylish, straight-through dress, perhaps paired with a swing jacket, seems to be the look.

Can you pick what the brand of clothing is? Or how much it cost? Unless it is from the latest season of a designer whose clothes you wear yourself, you probably have no idea. It is not something that is polite to ask, and it is not something appropriate to share. The value of the clothing lies more in how it is presented, and in the confidence of the wearer, than in a price tag.

Of course, if you are a man, it is possible that no-one notices what you wear at all. Karl Stefanovic wore the same inexpensive blue suit on Channel Nine's *Today* program for a year. Except on a few occasions where it was unavoidable, he wore it every day. He said that not a single audience member asked about it, with fashion commentators and other media appearing oblivious. He did, however, swap ties, so perhaps that's why no-one noticed. I wonder if a woman could do the same by wearing the same simple dress every day but putting on a different scarf or jacket.

INVEST IN CLASSIC PIECES

While I don't often buy clothes in mainstream shops, sometimes it is worth doing so to invest in a classic piece if it's good quality and makes you feel good. An example is a classic fitting suit made from good material. For around a decade I wore a black woollen suit that fit me perfectly. There was something about the cut that flattered me in all the right places, so I wore that until I pretty much wore it out. I remember spending more on it than I intended to, but I wore it on special occasions and I always felt good in it. I find it's always good to have at least one item that you feel you could wear to a job interview if you needed to (as I did with this outfit more than once), because you never know when an opportunity might arrive.

Similarly, I always like to have at least one formal gown in my wardrobe as you never know when you will need one. We had less than a week's notice about the ball in Antwerp. We had purchased Neil's tuxedo only a few weeks earlier, after finding it in an op shop while looking for something else. 'When are you ever going to wear that thing?' Neil's mum asked when he showed her a photo. They don't often wear tuxedos in the country area he came from, but as it turned out, he wore it soon after (and I thought he looked handsome!).

SECOND-HAND ROYALTY

There is absolutely nothing to be ashamed of when wearing second-hand clothes or clothes from a previous season. In fact, you will be in very good company.

Once upon a time, there was a stigma attached to wearing second-hand clothes, which is understandable, as giving clothes was often something you did to aid the poor. I remember reading historical novels that were set in pre-Victorian times. A wealthy woman would wear her clothes for perhaps one season, then she would pass her clothing on to her ladies' maid.

Some people still only wear items for one season, even though these days, clothing doesn't date as quickly. Even royalty wear clothing that is out of season or has been worn before. Some journalists criticised the Duchess of Cambridge for not buying a new outfit for Prince Harry and Meghan Markle's May 2018 wedding. Instead, she re-wore a pale-yellow Alexander McQueen coat, which several fashion reporters assessed was to avoid upstaging the bride.

It's not the first time that the Duchess of Cambridge has worn out of season clothing. The Duchess also wears and re-wears cheap clothing from time to time, earning her the nickname 'Thrifty Kate'. She wore a £38 polka-dot dress from Topshop to the opening of Warner Bros Studios in April 2013, and then wore it again a month later (while visibly pregnant) to attend a wedding. She has also been criticised for not supporting local designers because she wears clothes that are four years old — and which are often bought on sale.

The Duchess is not the only thrifty royal, with her father-in-law having a long history of thrifty dressing. His Royal Highness, the Prince of Wales, is, in addition to being the direct heir to the English throne, a successful business entrepreneur and artist in his own right. He presumably is not short of money. In a fashion interview with Marion Hume for the *Australian Financial Review*, he confessed that he often wore the same suit for many years, even decades — and was proud to do so because it would help the planet.

'I have always believed in trying to keep as many of my clothes and shoes going for as long as possible (some go back to 1971 and one jacket to 1969!) — through patches and repairs — and in this way I tend to be in fashion once every 25 years,' he said in the interview.

A long-time supporter of environmental causes, Prince Charles has also encouraged the re-emergence of demand for wool through his Campaign for Wool, amid his concerns about synthetics. He claims that his tailored suits have stood the test of time because they were made with quality wool. He believes consumers are increasingly rediscovering natural alternatives, particularly wool, that may cost a little more, but which last considerably longer. He describes the introduction of oil-based fibres in the 1960s and 1970s as 'the beginning of an environmental catastrophe,' as 'wool was substituted with polyester and acrylic as price triumphed over any ecological consideration'.

As such, Prince Charles was an early advocate for ethical fashion.

However, he is not alone as there is now a growing movement with many active supporters.

FASHION WITH A CONSCIENCE

Have you noticed the growing interest in 'vintage' clothing? In part, this reflects the beautiful and carefully considered styling involved in clothes from yesteryear. No 'one size fits all' mass-produced items from cheap jersey material, but rather items that were stitched with love and worn with pride.

Vintage dressing also reflects growing concerns about the ethical conditions under which many clothes are manufactured.

In 2013, the eight-story Rana Plaza building collapsed. The building in Dhaka, Bangladesh, housed thousands of mostly female textile workers. Brands produced in the building included Benetton, Mango and Walmart. The death toll from the incident was reported at 1135, with 2500 injured people rescued. Although this wasn't the first major safety incident involving a Bangladesh textiles factory, it captured international media attention and sparked an international conversation about the price of fashion, and greater awareness of where and how clothes are manufactured. It led to a global movement, Fashion Revolution Week, which encourages greater transparency in the fashion supply chain.

In addition to increased consciousness about the fashion supply chain, there is also a growing awareness of the environmental cost of clothing. According to a 2017 survey by YouGov, one in three Australians throw out clothes after only one wear. Most of these clothes go to landfill, with 75 per cent of Australians surveyed admitting that they have thrown away clothes in the last year. Older people are more likely to donate or recycle clothing, while younger generations are more likely to sell unwanted clothes online or burn them. More than 500,000 tonnes of textiles and leather are sent to landfill in Australia each year.

There has never been a better time to be proudly retro chic. Second hand is the new sustainable and ethical choice, and something you can wear with pride to work, on the red carpet or for any reason at all. An added advantage of vintage is that you are likely to be unique, and not have to face the awkwardness of bumping into someone else with the same dress at an event.

Now when people ask me where I got my outfit, I am proud to tell them not only that it is 'vintage', but that I bought it from my favourite op shop. And I'm not the only person to do so — I am finding that more and more people are thrilled to share with me their latest op shop finds. My mum also tells me that she recently met two fashionable ladies on the Gold Coast; when she complimented them on their outfits, they openly shared that they were charity shop finds. There was not a hint of embarrassment, and nor should there be.

CHEAP CLOTHING

An effective way to buy ethical and sustainable clothing is to source items second hand. I find this is often the cheapest way to shop as well. I love shopping at op shops, church fetes and other community events. I just love finding quirky bargains, and I also love shopping in these places because I know that my money is being invested into causes that I believe in.

I have several smaller op shops that I like to patronise, most of which are affiliated with churches and run by volunteers. I shop at larger op shops as well, including ones run by the St Vincent de Paul Society (Vinnies) and the Salvation Army (Salvos). However, I find the smaller shops often offer the best value and unexpected finds.

In recent years, items at some of the larger stores have become more expensive. I don't entirely blame op shop operators as, while the goods are donated, the stores have to spend money sorting and disposing of unwanted goods. The *Herald Sun* reported that dumping outside of Salvation Army stores costs it around $6 million a year to clean up. Several years ago, I visited a Vinnies sorting centre and warehouse to learn how the items were sorted and sold. Sorting the items dumped in front of stores is not only inconvenient but also a safety issue, with staff sometimes finding things like syringes or human excrement in amongst the waste.

However, I still find bargains at these mega-stores. Often, they will have sales to clear stock; they usually get inundated in spring and right after Christmas, when people are decluttering. Looking for colour-coded weekly specials is also cost-effective.

The hidden gems, however, are small op shops, which sometimes hide within churches. These often sell cheaper goods because they are run by volunteers and don't need to pay rent. If the church has an affluent congregation, it is likely to be an especially good source of items. There are three such church-run op shops in my neighbourhood—one even holds annual Christmas parties where they serve free champagne and snacks to shoppers as they browse. I don't know many boutiques that do that.

Charity second-hand sales are also a goldmine. There is a Zonta club in Canberra that hosts an annual fashion event, with money raised going to support women's initiatives such as birthing kits for Papua New Guinea. What I love about this is the community feel. In the group changeroom, the women often swap outfits—what doesn't suit one person often suits someone else. I go every year with a girlfriend, and we have a wonderful time shopping and chatting.

I have bought some nice outfits from garage sales, but not as often as from op shops. It is often difficult to try on clothing for one thing, and for another, it is rarely displayed well. The exception is the time I bought three fabulous vintage-style Lindy Bop dresses from a lady who had a retro fashion sense I related to.

I love looking at second-hand clothes online, such as through Facebook Marketplace. However, I must admit I have never bought anything — not once. I find that the prices charged are generally higher than op shops, and you have to drive a long way just to see one item. I did, however, scour for wedding dresses and, had I wanted a big designer princess froo froo gown, I am sure I could have found one at a fraction of the price of a new dress.

SPRING'S BOUTIQUE — SWISHING WITH THE BEST

I have the best sister in the world. Well, I am a tad biased, but I think my sister, Spring, is very cool and incredibly good to me. She also has an amazing wardrobe, and she is short like me and of a similar build. When we get together, we like to swap clothes.

It's a bit of a ritual and something of a family tradition. I remember my aunts coming to visit us in Queensland, and the sisters rummaging through my mum's wardrobe and trying on clothes. Although they have unique styles, there were always things they liked and appreciated. They gossiped at a hundred miles an hour, commenting on who looked best in the outfits, and it was so much more fun than trying on clothing under harsh fluorescent lights in a lonely change room.

When my sister and I get together, it's a similar scene. We usually start with afternoon tea and a bit of a gossip at her home in the Gold Coast hinterland. Then the topic turns to fashion.

'Do you want to look at some clothes?' my sister will ask, with a glint of excitement in her eyes.

'Sure,' I say. Then we go to her room and rifle through her extensive wardrobe, where she picks out things for me to try on. Spring has some amazing clothes and, like me, she loves op shopping and has some unique pieces. She also has a real eye for picking out clothes that are wearable and look good together. Spring understands fashion brands, and she understands intuitively what will look slimming and fashionable on me. She has a way of encouraging me to try on styles or combinations that I would not have thought of myself.

Meanwhile, I pull out items that I have brought up from Canberra for Spring to try. On more than one occasion, I have walked into her house wearing an outfit and when I have left she is wearing it — we have done a total swap, with my suitcase bulging full of clothes gifted from her. I don't have as many items to give, but so far I have a good track record of picking items that she is likely to wear. One yellow patterned dress, with a matching amber necklace, is something that she tells me always elicits comments. It looks much better on her than it did on me, and even though I loved wearing it, I am so happy that it is now hers.

All the time we chat and giggle and talk about where we are going to wear these outfits and about life in general. We have a little fashion parade as we go, showing off the outfits and what we look like in them. It's much more fun than shopping in an ordinary shop, and the customer service is much better. I also come away with the validation of knowing that my sister, whose judgement I trust, thinks something looks good on me. (She tells me honestly if something doesn't work.) A few years ago, I nicknamed this experience 'Spring's Boutique'.

While my sister and I have been doing this for years, we are part of a growing trend of swapping clothing and accessories (and sometimes even books and furniture). It even has a name — swishing.

Swishing means to rustle, as in silk, as in getting so excited about a new find that your friend has that it rustles away like silk. The term swishing was coined by Lucy Shea of Futerra Sustainability Communications when she created eco-friendly clothes swapping experiences. In the UK, the swishing movement was popularised over a decade ago when Twiggy and Lauren Laverne championed it through a *Twiggy's Frock Exchange* series on the BBC.

Swishing events can be anything from a large, formal event—often in aid of a charity—where you pay a fee to attend and must bring some items to exchange, to what my sister and I regularly do, to something between friends. Years ago, pre-kids, I hosted a swishing get-together of other frugal ladies (the Frugalista Sistas). We were all different shapes and sizes, but there was plenty for us to share with one another. Even one of my friends who was a few sizes larger than everyone else in the group (and who had expressed reservations about finding anything that would fit her) went home with several outfits and accessories. There is always something for everyone.

GOING WITHOUT NEW CLOTHES FOR A YEAR

In 2014, I decided not to buy any clothes for a year. In late 2013, I had done an inventory of all our belongings for insurance purposes. We were moving back to Australia after three and a half years in Taiwan. I was shocked.

I looked at my coats (more than ten, including ones meant for arctic temperatures), shoes (lost count), cardigans, jumpers, dresses and evening wear. I allocated a conservative value based on what it would cost to replace our possessions at full value, just in case everything got lost. While rare, it is indeed possible to lose all your worldly goods en route, and if you are in that situation, you rarely have the option of buying things second hand or cheaply because you need to replace them quickly.

When I tallied up what was there and, based on the full replaceable value, my family's clothing came to a total of $30,000. That was a lower-end value.

Admittedly, most of my clothes were given to us, or bought on sale at the morning markets (aka the wet markets) or at op shops in Australia. We seemed to have a lot of stuff—or at least I did. Surely most women have a lot of clothes? Wanting a second opinion, I went to our lovely Filipino maid (those were the days when I had household help!) for a second opinion.

'Do I have a lot of clothes?' I asked.

She laughed nervously, then confidently looked me in the face and answered, 'Yes, ma'am, you have a LOT of clothes.'

So then and there, I stopped buying new clothes for 12 months — except when I really needed to. The idea was to downsize and learn to appreciate what I had.

As it happened, 2014 was a year of extreme fiscal constraint. My ex-husband and I returned to Australia just as the rental market in Canberra dropped dramatically. As we had rental properties, this hit us hard. We also had significant vacancies — in one case as long as six months.

Then in August that year, I ended the marriage.

Having the challenge of not buying new clothes was a good way to justify why I was not spending money. I made up for it in 2015. Whenever something stressful happened to do with my ex, such as mediation or meetings to discuss property settlement, I would go and buy myself a new op shop frock afterwards. I did not splurge per se, but having gone without new clothes for a year I enjoyed buying a few treats.

However, during the 2014 challenge it was in a sense easier than I thought to go without new clothes. And I did learn to appreciate and value what I had.

Through that year, I discovered new things in my wardrobe and experimented with new combinations. I tried to wear a different outfit to work every day for over a month — and I almost succeeded. However, even if I did wear repeat outfits, who would have cared? As noted earlier, if I was a man, probably no-one would have noticed at all.

Could you imagine if people said things like, 'Oh, look at Fred. He's wearing that paisley purple tie *again*. Didn't he wear that last Monday?'

It never happens. It never happens because unless you are wearing something outrageous like a safari suit, people don't notice. (I did, in fact, have a boss who liked to wear a safari suit in summer, and it was much commented on, but even then, I lost count after the first few times he wore it into the office.)

If you change to a new job, or if you move overseas as I did, no-one would have seen your 'old' clothes anyway. To them, every day is a new day where you are wearing new clothes. It is only you that notices and thinks about how you feel in them.

How did I survive on a 'no new clothes for a year' challenge?

- I accepted with gratitude some clothing from my sister. I figured that swishing was fine on this challenge. The weird thing was that I had planned to bend the 'no new clothes' rule by buying a pair of black pants—something I deemed a necessity—only for Spring to gift me exactly what I had planned to buy. She must have read my mind.

- I found a black pashmina, discarded by somebody at my long-neglected workstation in my new position. Like the black pants, I had planned to buy one and then it turned up …

- I bought new undies (only to find they were too small!). A friend shared an ad on Facebook about a couples' retreat that suggested your marriage was in trouble 'if you no longer wear sexy underwear'. I, therefore, classed new underwear as an essential item.

- I bought a warm scarf, beanie and gloves from a Salvos op shop. I had been living in sub-tropical Taiwan so I needed warm clothing, and I classed this as being in the 'cold weather emergency' category. But to be honest, I could have made use of my new black pashmina as it was perfectly fine.

- I bought an aqua-marine silk scarf and lots of (op-shop) jewellery. I didn't include jewellery in my 'do not buy' list, but I've got no excuse for the scarf. I just liked it (and I did wear it several times that year).

During my challenge, there were times when I felt dowdy. In my blogging life, I met several cool fashionistas, including dedicated fashion bloggers. My work colleagues were always so impeccably dressed. In comparison, I felt like my wardrobe was dull and staid. I wondered if my confidence would be augmented if I wore something new, or reduced my weight by 15 kg. However, I still receive comments on items of clothing I was wearing back then. The issue wasn't with my clothes, but what I projected when wearing them. It's all about attitude—a signature brooch here, dangly earrings there, an elegant scarf and a 'hold yourself up and be proud' approach. I am learning to affirm out loud every day that 'I love and approve of myself'. Having lots of new and expensive clothes doesn't necessarily translate into enhanced self-worth and style.

FRUGALISTA CHALLENGE

Do not buy any new clothes or shoes for a month. This includes op shop clothes, handbags, scarves and accessories. Make do with what you have, or swap with others. And share Facebook and Instagram photos so that we can see how fabulous you look! Feel free to use the hashtag #joyfulfrugalista.

Best-ever hand treatment

Try this for a frugal day spa at home—it costs approximately 10c. The salt helps remove any rough or dead skin.

½ teaspoon olive oil

½ teaspoon salt

> Pour the olive oil onto one hand, then sprinkle on the salt. Rub your hands together, massaging the oil and salt into your skin. Rinse off with warm water, then dry your hands on a hand towel.

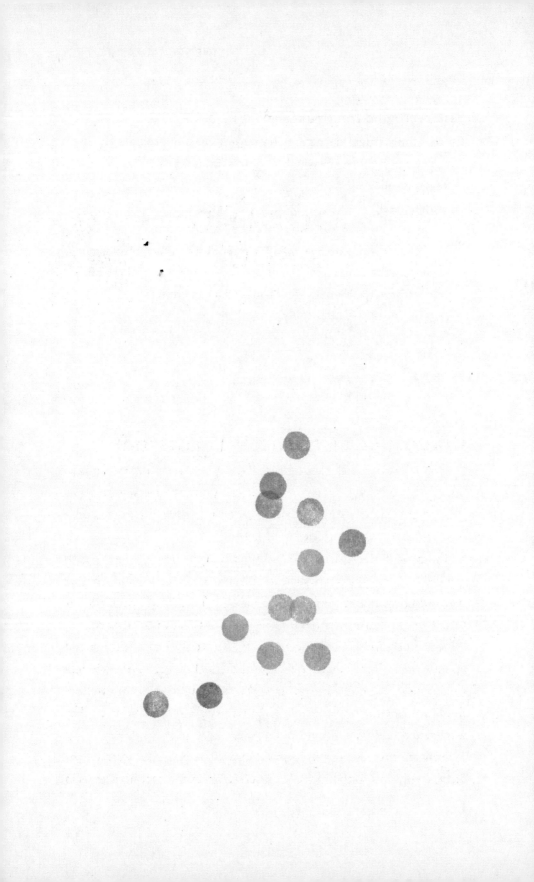

CHAPTER 6

OUT AND ABOUT

Saving on transport

THE COMING DISRUPTION IN TRANSPORT

Do you love your car? Have you ever sat down and worked out how much you really pay for transport? Is your car more of a chariot than a means of transportation? Do you have too many cars? And does your bike sit idle in your garage?

I want to disrupt your thinking about transportation. I want you to think about how you get from A to B (and C and then D) and whether there are cheaper and more environmentally friendly ways of doing so. I want you to be aware of the changes that are already taking place.

Since the early twentieth century, humans have had a fixation and fascination with the automobile. It transformed modern life: no longer were people constrained to living within walking or horse or even rail distance from their workplace. They were free to live wherever they wanted and to drive to wherever they wanted to go.

New suburbs sprung up. People moved out of what were (then) dirty, smelly and sometimes even diseased inner metropolitan areas in favour of the promise of a backyard, parks and vast expanses of space. People went on Sunday drives and picnics. We all travelled a lot more, zooming around everywhere.

However, the car as we know it is changing. Global warming means that many countries have signed up to the Paris Agreement to limit emissions. Cars, whether running on petrol or diesel or even ethanol, produce a lot of emissions, so manufacturers are looking at ways to make them run more efficiently.

Enter the electric vehicle. Electric vehicles are currently, for the most part, expensive luxury vehicles. Mass commercial uptake of electric vehicles has not yet occurred, but it is only a matter of time.

Added to this is a concurrent trend: automated vehicles (AVs). Several major tech and car companies are investing heavily in automated vehicles. Despite the killing of a woman in Arizona by an Uber automated vehicle on trial, AV trials are going full steam ahead.

The car of the future is likely to look very different to the car you currently drive. It probably won't use petrol and will need to be recharged at every stop. You won't need to park it, because you can use your mobile phone to get your car to pick you up at any time. It can go home to wait for you, or maybe you'll even share it among several people.

Public transport is also likely to increase in popularity. Urbanisation, including in Asia, will mean there are more and more people living in big cities. There is greater investment in infrastructure like high-speed rail, subways, light rail and even buses that are really automated vehicles. Emissions reduction goals will also make investment in public transport attractive.

Sound futuristic? Well, some of these things are happening already. Later in this chapter I'll explore concepts such as car sharing and ridesharing. But for now, I want to plant the seed in your mind that disruption in transportation is coming, and that can mean huge savings for frugalistas.

HOW MUCH DOES YOUR CAR ACTUALLY COST YOU?

You may love your car, but do you really need it? Can you really afford it? Do you even know how much it is costing you?

On my blog, I examined the role of the car during a transport challenge. My aim was to see whether our family could survive with only one car. I was already cycling to work several days a week, but after the challenge I decided I didn't really need my own car anymore. The end result was that I decided to give up my car.

Let me explain.

After Neil and I became engaged, the topic of cars came up more and more in conversation. We were both rebuilding financially after divorce, and we also had a problem: it was hard to park two cars (one an SUV and the second a dual-cab ute) in the tandem carparking spaces in the underground carpark in my apartment complex.

Prior to meeting me, Neil lived in the country, which explains why he has a large Isuzu D-Max ute, a post-separation mid-life crisis motorbike, and a caravan. In contrast, I came to the relationship with a 17-year-old Toyota RAV4 that was still going strong (but not likely to be for much longer), and a collection of bicycles (two kids' bikes, a Giant Cypress hybrid bike, an electric bike and an old men's bike that my dad used when he visited).

Owning a car wasn't terribly important to me. I'm not really into cars in a major way and never have been. I wasn't even that into my ex-boyfriend's shiny new red M Series BMW; sometimes I got car sick. I didn't get my driver's licence until I was 31, and even after that I rarely drove my car as I'm a nervous driver and was much happier being a passenger. For years my ex-husband and I only had one car. (At times we had more than one, but I convinced him to cut back.) It was a bit of a struggle to coordinate after we had kids, but we made it work.

In early 2016, I realised that I needed to re-examine the way my life was designed. I was commuting to work each day, doing a 20 km commute morning and night, that involved dropping off and picking up the kids at two different places. It was manageable, and compared to life in big cities, nothing to complain about. However, it was stressful when I got stuck in traffic or was late leaving work due to urgent deadlines.

Spending so much time commuting meant that I had less time for exercise. I was usually exhausted by the time I got home, and that was before I even started making dinner, doing the dishes, making lunches for the next day, getting kids in pyjamas, reading stories, etc., etc., etc. My butt was getting bigger and my car was making clunking sounds.

So, I sold my house and moved to an inner-city apartment, where my kids were walking distance from school and my work was cycling distance away. Arguably, I didn't even need a car anymore, except that sometimes I did drive, such as to church on Sunday, to meet friends, to do the shopping, or when it was raining or I felt too lazy to cycle. I couldn't really cycle with the kids out to visit Neil's family in the country, and as part of the trip is on an unsealed dirt road, we also need a solid car to drive there.

Many of us are accustomed to thinking of the car as a necessity. We are accustomed to believing that we 'need' that vehicle. 'It's not a car, it's a CHARIOT!' my dad once told me when I mentioned that my ex-husband wanted to buy a car when we were in Taiwan (even though we lived in the central commercial district).

This attitude is a result, in part, of many of us living in far-flung suburbs and thinking we can't get around without a car. That used to be my reality, too. And more than that, a car represents freedom and independence. Obtaining your licence and then getting your first car is a rite of passage for many young people.

However, things are changing. Public transport is improving, there are more options to work from home, and as supplies of fossil fuels reduce, petrol (or even diesel) prices are likely to go up. And people (like me) are moving back into urban city centres as the areas embrace urban renewal and become more liveable. Uber and other rideshare programs are making short-term chauffeured rides more affordable, and car-sharing arrangements are becoming more accessible too.

What does this all mean for car ownership? A major consideration is that it costs a lot just to own a car, whether you drive it out of your garage or not. It is difficult to generalise as there are so many variables depending on make, model and age of car and registration costs in different states and territories. However, based on my own experience, here is a snapshot of how much I saved by giving up my car.

- **Registration.** My rego cost me almost $1000 per year. This is a rate set by the relevant government authorities, but generally the larger the car, the more you pay.

- **Insurance.** I had to take out compulsory third party insurance, which covers damage to another car or person. In addition, I always take out full comprehensive insurance that also covers me for theft, fire and other damage. My combined annual insurance premiums were around $1000.

- **Servicing and repairs.** My 17-year-old Toyota required $1500 in servicing and repairs in the months before I gave it up. This would vary depending on the car—older cars usually require more care and servicing.

- **Car battery.** On average a car battery lasts five to seven years. (I found that out the hard way on a cold winter's night around two years ago—Canberra's cold winters really reduce battery life.) It costs around $120 for a new battery, so on average that's $17 to $24 a year.

- **Roadside assistance.** This is useful to have when your battery runs out and for all sorts of other reasons. I used my roadside assistance three times within a year, so my $110 annual fee was a good investment.

  Total: at least $3627 a year. This equates to $9.94 per day, just to have my car sitting in my garage. If you actually drive your car regularly, it will obviously cost you more.

- **Petrol.** If I drove my car an average of 20,000 km a year, I would spend $3062.80 a year on petrol (assuming I'm paying $1.55 a litre for fuel). You can mitigate this by filling up with cheaper fuel, e.g. at Costco, or by using vouchers or petrol cards associated with leased vehicles.

- **Parking.** I used to have free car parking at work, but it now costs $14 a day. Assuming I paid $14, five days a week for 48 weeks a year, that's $3360 in parking a year.

Running costs: $6422.80. This works out at $8.39 a day just on petrol, or $17.60 a day including parking.

So my car was costing me just over $10,000 a year. And that's without other expenses that I could expect from time to time.

- **Tyres.** Tyres will cost you around $250 each and last around 60,000 to 80,000 km. Accordingly, you will need to pay $1000 every three to four years, so you can expect to pay an average of $250 a year.

- **Car washing.** For the car proud, this could add at least $10 to $20 a month or even a week.

- **Accidents.** They happen! It might just be a little dent, a ding with a shopping trolley or a bad parking job in your garage. It might be a more serious collision with another car. It might not even be your fault. If it requires an insurance claim, you'll need to pay the excess and you might lose your no claim bonus. Or you might choose to live with the damage and accept that it will reduce the value of your car.

And it doesn't end there! Here are some more factors that can drastically increase what your car is costing you.

- **Car repayments.** The best way to pay for your car is to save up for it. The second-best financing method is to make a withdrawal from your mortgage and then make higher repayments to compensate (if your mortgage is for 25 to 30 years, over time you will pay a lot more unless you pay extra). Based on a $40,000 car loan and a rate of 8 per cent (my research indicates rates are between 6 and 8 per cent), expect to pay $633 a month over seven years, which is a total of $7596 a year and $53,172 over the life of the loan.

- **Depreciation.** Unless you have a rare collectible vehicle, your car will depreciate significantly in value. Enjoy that new car smell because you are paying for the privilege. A new car will generally depreciate between 30 per cent and 50 per cent in the first three or four years. Assuming you spend $40,000 on a new SUV or family car, that would mean you would lose between $12,000 and $20,000 in depreciation in four years — on average this would amount to between $3000 and $5000 year.

- **Class of vehicle.** If you drive a luxury car, many of the costs could be much higher than for a modest car, including petrol (if the car requires premium fuel), insurance, servicing, repairs and repayments. My dad's second-hand Mercedes required $5000 for suspension airbags last year — usually European and luxury models cost more.

Neil found this out the hard way when he accidentally backed into a BMW and damaged the plastic grille — it cost $1500 to replace.

- **Age.** Younger people generally pay much more for insurance as they don't have a driving history and insurance companies consider them to be a higher risk. A person under 25 years of age driving a performance vehicle can expect to pay in excess of $2000 for full comprehensive insurance.

The big question is whether your car is worth what it costs you. Do you have a second car that you aren't using that you could consider selling? Or could you, in the interests of getting ahead financially, get by without owning a car at all?

LEASING VERSUS BUYING

I want to briefly touch on the issue of how to buy a car. I have the option through work to salary sacrifice to 'buy' a car, provided it is a new vehicle or a vehicle that is under two years of age. The arrangement works on a leasing system.

The company that manages the salary sacrificing arrangement on behalf of my work does a brisk business with this scheme. I suspect it is much more popular than other products they offer, such as salary sacrificing for superannuation. Salary sacrificing is a system whereby your employer allows you to pay for some items from your pre-tax salary, which reduces your taxable income and therefore leads to money saving.

My ex-husband wanted to buy a new car at one stage and argued that, because of the salary sacrificing, it would be cheaper than keeping our existing car. When I did the sums at that point I concluded that we would not, in fact, be saving money. However, it depends on many variables.

Neil is nearing the end of a salary sacrificing lease arrangement for his ute. Since he has actually leased, and as he is crunching numbers with a view to purchasing a new vehicle next year (one that we can use to tow a caravan, and one I can actually drive), I asked him for his insights. He said that leasing can be beneficial because you get the tax advantage of paying via salary sacrificing. You can make additional savings by paying pre-tax dollars on fuel, maintenance, registration and running costs.

Another advantage is that many companies that run leasing options have good relationships with car dealerships and can negotiate a good price. Obviously, if you are a good negotiator in your own right you might not need them to do this for you, but every little bit helps.

A leasing arrangement works best for people on higher incomes. But according to Neil, the advantages are not as good as they used to be because you need to pay fringe benefits tax if you drive more than 15,000 km a year.

In Neil's experience, you don't get a choice of finance companies and often they charge rates that are slightly higher than other lenders. Also, there is a monthly fee that you need to pay to the leasing company. And you don't get to choose where you fill up with petrol.

You might not own your car, but you still have to pay out the residual value on the car when the lease term is up. The residual value goes down dramatically towards the end of the fixed lease period, which makes it financially disadvantageous to sell your car early. People's lives change: you might suddenly get a job overseas, or go back to full-time study, or have children and need a people mover. As such it can sometimes cause a problem if you're locked into a leasing arrangement.

Every situation is different and, if you are considering a leasing arrangement, you should crunch the numbers and compare various deals. Neil has eventually concluded that when we replace his ute, it will be better to withdraw from the mortgage so that we get a lower interest rate. This will, however, only be better if we commit to making much higher repayments on our mortgage. The interest rate might be lower, but it is spread out over many years, so over time the car will cost us a lot more unless we pay it off sooner.

THE RISE OF CAR-SHARING SCHEMES

Canberra is car city. For decades it had some of the best roads in Australia. Many of them go in circles—I'm not sure what that says about our city's culture—but they are generally well maintained and easy to drive on. That has been a good thing because traditionally we have not had good public transport infrastructure.

Being a 'car city' dweller, I was slow to recognise the growth in the car-sharing movement. However, on a weekend trip to Sydney, we noticed car-share vehicles parked along a road in Potts Point (near Kings Cross). Along the tight roads lined with historic townhouses and apartments (some used for recreational and not just residential purposes, many busier later at night—enough said), we couldn't help but notice the rows of car-share vehicles.

'What a good idea,' Neil remarked. 'This must be perfect for people living in inner-city apartments who don't have space to park their cars. No worry about getting a parking ticket this way.'

We paused to admire the cars, all functional vehicles. We wondered how they operated.

I thought it was just a Sydney thing. Then several months later I noticed some car-share vehicles within walking distance of my home. Then we noticed more of them during a daytrip to Wollongong, including what looked like people out on a daytrip from Sydney. Then Neil noticed more vans at IKEA.

I began to get interested. Could this be the answer to the dilemma of the tight parking spaces in my apartment block? Or what to do when my

17-year-old car reached the end of its life? Or the end of having to take time off work (or begging to work from home for the day) so that I could get my car serviced?

There are two major companies that operate car-sharing schemes in Australia: GoGet and Popcar. Large cities such as London embraced the concept earlier, with companies such as Zipcar becoming ubiquitous in tight urban areas.

It's a clever idea. As much as many of us might think that we can go totally carless, sometimes you just want the security of knowing that you can access a car from time to time. You might want to drive into the country for a daytrip, or go somewhere where there isn't good public transport, or buy more shopping than will fit into a bicycle basket. You might even want to use a different type of vehicle, e.g. a ute or van for larger purchases.

I recently trialled using a GoGet vehicle. I had given my car to my dad and wanted another option to use when Neil was away or couldn't drive, or when I needed to go somewhere too far to cycle (or if I had my kids with me).

I liked it so much that I now have a GoGet membership. I signed up online, was issued with a swipe card in the mail, and now I can book and use a car when I need one. I first used it when I took Neil to hospital for a heart procedure. I was a bit nervous (as I've said, I am a nervous driver), but I quickly discovered that it was all super-easy.

Booking a car is simple. You go online and choose one based on the day, time and make of vehicle. I have since downloaded the GoGet app and find that it is even easier to use. There are two pods close to home that I like to use. I just walk to the car, wave the smart card over the window shield, get in, adjust the seat and mirrors, turn the key in the ignition and I am away!

I am often amazed at how easy it all is. The Toyota Corollas in the pods near me are a newer model, they're clean and in good condition and I don't have to do anything other than drive them. There's even a petrol card I can use to fill up the car.

Being a frugalista, I really wanted to know how much I could save. According to GoGet's analysis (and based on a number of assumptions), a moderate car user driving a mid-range vehicle would save between $4758 and over $9000 in a year by using one of its cars rather than owning a car outright.

Of course, the savings depend on the distance you drive and where you live. If you lived in a rural area and drove long distances—as Neil used to—something like a car-share vehicle is probably not the right option for you. For one thing, there probably aren't any 'pods' of cars nearby like there are near my inner-city apartment.

If you were planning a weekend away or a work trip that involved driving long distances, you could still be better off with a rental car. Neil, for instance, can get competitive corporate rates on rental cars through his work. He estimates that it often only costs him $90 to drive from Canberra to Sydney using a hire car.

The advantage of signing up for a car-sharing arrangement is that it is quick and easy to use. If you need a car for an hour or two, you don't need to go to a hire car company and do all the paperwork. A few clicks on an app, a short walk, and you're in your car.

Another advantage is that a car-sharing arrangement gives you access to a wide range of vehicles. GoGet have vans, utes, SUVs, Kia people movers and even new model Audi vehicles.

The big selling point for me is that car-sharing arrangements free you from the drudgery of car maintenance. To be honest, I am clueless when it comes to car maintenance. I would have no idea if my car was leaking oil, if the suspension had a problem or even if it was about to blow up. In the last 18 months I have had thick black smoke coming out of the bonnet of my car, broken down and needed to replace a radiator, and had a seriously flat (i.e. dead) battery. NRMA roadside assistance is my best friend. Car-sharing companies not only take care of maintenance, but pay registration, insurance, purchase and sell cars, clean and wash them, and attend to smash repairs.

THE UBER REVOLUTION

Canberra was the first place in Australia to legalise Uber. But Canberrans are definitely not the only ones that enjoy Uber now. The Uber revolution has innovated transportation by making rideshare easy and accessible. Even my parents now 'Uber' to places. And my kids just love going via Uber; it's a special treat for them.

The rise of ridesharing has changed how many people plan their social lives. People are more willing to go out and about to restaurants, cafes and bars and just 'Uber' home if they have had too much to drink or if it's late. For people like me who live in inner-city areas, the cost and convenience of getting an Uber to take you somewhere now has to be weighed up against the cost and convenience of owning a car.

In recent months I have also watched the rapid advances of related companies such as UberEats and Deliveroo, which have revolutionised takeaway food options. You can now even have McDonald's delivered, something that would have seemed inconceivable not that long ago.

Innovations such as automated vehicles and competing brands, including Lyft and niche services catered to women, are shaking up the ridesharing space here and overseas. Although Uber is a newcomer, there are already predictions that it might be superseded if it is not agile enough to respond to changing circumstances. And it still hasn't been legalised in many jurisdictions. Whatever happens, we have experienced that Uber moment. Our concept of transportation has been disrupted. We now begin to talk about transport trips in terms of how much it would cost to take an Uber, the Uber distance metric. We are also beginning to think about car ownership in different ways.

CASE STUDY

HOW JOHN GAVE UP HIS SECOND CAR AND PAID OVER $8000 OFF HIS MORTGAGE

John is a work friend, and although we have never actually worked together, I feel like I know him well. He and his wife rented my home when I was on posting in Taipei. They were good tenants, and my neighbours were all sad to see them go (luckily the neighbours were also happy to have me back!).

A few years ago, John spotted me hovering under a plum tree across the road from our work building. Ornamental prunus have been planted widely in Canberra and in spring they blossom into a profusion of pink candyfloss-coloured delights. In early summer they produce small, tart, cherry-like fruit that the birds love, but which otherwise make a mess on the footpaths. I was foraging for the small plums in the tree when John saw me. After politely inquiring about what I was doing (I must have looked odd picking fruit in my corporate work clothes), we got to talking about my frugal blog and my frugal lifestyle.

Six months later I bumped into John again. 'I've been reading your blog,' he said. 'And, inspired by your story about paying off your mortgage, my wife and I have decided to focus on doing the same.'

They had bought their dream home a few years previously, when they moved out of my house. Like most young couples, they took on a large mortgage that seemed unsurmountable.

John's strategy involved selling their second car. 'We didn't really need it that much. It was there in case my wife needed to go out when I wasn't there. But then I did the sums and realised that even if she spent $50 a week in taxis or Uber rides, we would still be a long way ahead.'

As it happened, they didn't need the second car nearly as much as they thought. John took up cycling to work and got fitter, leaving their one car at home for his wife to use.

Over the course of two years, John and his wife saved at least $5724 by not running their second car. This consisted of rego ($1000), insurance ($300), maintenance ($500) and fuel at $20/week ($1040). They also earnt $2500 from the sale of their second car. This came to $8224, which they used to reduce their mortgage.

WALKING IS THE BEST MEDICINE

'Shall we go for a long walk, or a long walk?' my dad is fond of saying. He is 74 years old and in excellent health. He recently returned from a week-long skiing trip in Japan, and after that he went on a hiking trip to Mt Hotham (with side trips cycling on the Alpine rail trails in northern Victoria). In Japan, he and his mate got lost skiing off-piste, but thankfully they found their way back.

Taking long walks or cycling every morning is one of my dad's secrets to keeping fit and vibrant. He also credits his lunchtime walks when he was still working with helping him to overcome depression and anxiety. I have adopted his habit and now I also go for a quick walk around the block whenever I feel stressed and need to clear my head. I don't think it is a coincidence that there are many walk and talk support groups, including for women recovering from domestic violence. Even Buddha used walking as a form of meditation; there is a certain rhythm to walking that is soothing to the soul.

I was talking to my dear dad about how I planned to talk about walking in this book. He reminded me that your health is the most important thing that you have in this life, and that walking is one of the best ways to stay fit and healthy.

'I've just come back from a trip with a lot of wealthy people,' he said. 'Some of them are worth four, maybe five million dollars. One couple there were around ten years younger than me. But they don't live active lifestyles. They drive everywhere rather than walk. They have so many health problems. All they do is talk about their illnesses and the medications they are on. I'm comparatively much fitter and healthier. As you grow older, the quality of your life becomes even more dependent on your health, and this is something that money can't buy.'

Human beings are designed to walk. There is something about walking that takes us back to our prehistoric, nomadic, cave-dwelling roots. Walking is natural and normal for many people, and something that healthy people often take for granted.

As walking is a load-bearing exercise, it helps improve bone density. It can help people reduce weight (it was my secret weapon when I shed 13 kg after the birth of my eldest son). It is also one of the few exercises that solves more injuries than it causes. When recovering from a heart attack, regular walking every day was one of the top forms of exercise that Neil was encouraged to do.

So why is it that we seem to do anything we can to avoid walking? Why is it that we drive to the corner store rather than walk? How often do we drive to the gym, only to spend 20 to 30 minutes walking on a treadmill?

Around 15 years ago I had a gym membership. It was a bit of a splurge for someone who had only just graduated from university, but I was overweight, didn't feel good about myself and I felt that I needed to do something. At that time, I was working in a job that I loved. It was not especially stressful. I know that the trend these days is to complain that your work is so busy, and that you work such long hours, but at that time I was just in my groove and things flowed simply and easily. After work I would travel by bus across town to the gym.

When I got to the gym, things became stressful. I had to get there early to get a locker as there weren't enough. There was a crowd of women in the change room. The music was loud and overpowering. I felt self-conscious in the exercise class; I didn't really enjoy it but was toughing it out. By the time I got home it was dark and I was tired. I would sometimes mindlessly overeat.

Then one day, I stopped and thought about what I was doing. Outside it was a sunny spring afternoon verging on sunset. 'Why don't I go for a walk instead?' I asked myself. I could get off the bus one stop earlier, saving $2 each way. The walk from the bus station in the central district to my house wove around a lake, and it was scenic.

When I decided to go for walks rather than sweating it out in the gym, I immediately saved around $1000 a year (it was a boutique gym; these days it would cost around double that). I also felt an immediate sense of relief; I was calmer and happier when I did more walking. It helped me to process my thoughts and to think through problems differently. I also wasted less time on the bus or driving to the gym, and less time changing in and out of clothes and showering. As such, I found that I walked (and thereby exercised) more often.

After that experience, I made a point of walking whenever I could. I especially liked to go walking on a Saturday morning to my local ALDI supermarket. I would take a shopping bag or a backpack and do most of my shopping that way. I didn't buy everything for the week, but often bought the major things. Yes, it was heavy, especially as the way home was uphill. But knowing that I had to carry everything home made me less likely to buy things I didn't need. I told myself that carrying a heavy shopping bag was no different from lifting weights at the gym.

ON YOUR BIKE!

Money blogger Peter Adeney, aka Mr Money Mustache, famously advocates ditching your car and instead cycling everywhere. I remember when I first started reading his posts, I thought, 'Yeah, that sounds really good, but …'.

I had dreams of using my electric bike to get to work, but then my kids were offered a rare place in the childcare centre at my work. I know some people who can cycle 20+ kilometres on hilly routes with young children, but it was a bit too much for me.

When I calculate the move from outer suburbia to inner city in terms of dollars and cents, I am not yet clear if there is a discernible benefit. I had paid off the mortgage on my home, and I had rent coming in from my granny flat. But I am making savings in transport and energy. More importantly, I believe that moving to an area where I can lead a more active life is adding years to my life.

I have been cycling to work regularly for over a year. Since I started, my health and energy levels have really improved. This is not just in my imagination: my dad noticed it when we went skiing together last year. I am not a super-fit person, I have no dreams of being a triathlete and I struggle with my weight. If I can cycle to work, anyone can.

That said, whether or not I am financially better off after moving to a more expensive area, I do save money on transport, and when I tallied it all up, I was surprised by just how much I am saving.

How much do I save by cycling? Apart from the money saved on parking and by taking showers at work, I have saved $20 a week by cancelling my pool membership at a hotel near work (for two years my luxurious treat was swimming once or twice a week). Also, even when I was only cycling three days a week, I began to notice a dramatic decrease in my petrol consumption. I estimate I saved at least $100 on petrol every month.

I also extended the time between car services by around nine months; because I wasn't using my car as much, there was much less mileage. This saved me around $1000 on servicing for my older car, and probably saved me around $1000 in depreciation of the vehicle as I was doing much less mileage.

This is how much my savings stacked up:

Parking ($14 a day for 48 weeks)	$3360
Swimming pool membership savings	$1040
Petrol savings	$1200
Depreciation	$1000
Servicing fees	$1000
Hot water savings	$150
Total:	**$7750**

To this, I would add that my health and immune system over the last year have been better than they have ever been. While everyone at work was down with the flu, I was healthy. (Of course, I am not totally immune: after bragging about how I never get colds anymore I suddenly got sick late last year.) I needed significantly fewer sick days last year because, overall, I had fewer colds and viruses. I have generous sick leave provisions with my job, but when I'm sick, I spend more than I would like on doctors' visits and medicines, and I don't have as many home-cooked meals as I would like. Because I need to rest, I also have less energy for money saving or earning activities in general.

My second-hand Giant bike cost $320. It was in great condition and didn't need much servicing. I have had a few flat tyres, which Neil has fixed for me. He tells me it would help if I didn't ride over sharp bindies.

Inspired by me, Neil recently bought his own bike. My apartment is close to several bike paths, and we enjoy weekend rides together.

When I ride my bike rather than drive a car, I have a unique perspective on the world. I am blessed to live in Canberra, a beautiful city, and to cycle past many national institutions as part of my daily commute. I drive past them, too, but when I am driving I am more focused on the traffic than on the view. I see things differently, and while puffing up and over bridges is not that much fun, I arrive at work with a lot more positive energy than when I drive.

I live 6.5 km from work (7 km if I take a scenic route). First, I cycle with my kids to school. It's a bit hard to get them out the door, and then they wobble on their bikes. They are unsure of themselves, but thankfully they attend a school that encourages cycling. In a few years they will be able to cycle to school by themselves. I keep reminding myself that taking the time now to cycle with them of a morning is giving them skills that they will use for life. Most mornings I struggle to hide my impatience when I know I am running late for work!

PUBLIC TRANSPORT

Until recently, the prospect of using public transport regularly was as exciting as … well, let's be honest, it wasn't very exciting at all. However, there is disruption coming in the public transport space to rival what is happening in other transport sectors.

When I lived in Taipei, I loved using the Mass Rapid Transport (MRT) underground train system. So did my kids. It cost less than AUD$1, and there was a train from the stop next to my work every two minutes. It was quick and easy to get around, especially when all you had to do was swipe your EasyCard (which you could also use for purchases at convenience stores and many other places).

I did not use the buses as often, but when I did they were also of a high standard. They had TVs, they were clean, there was a handy website that helped you navigate which bus to use, and the bus stations had electronic signage. It was even cheaper than the MRT system.

I also found that because of the good public transport system, I walked and cycled a lot more when I lived in Taipei—a city of 2.7 million people—than when I returned to suburban Canberra. Millions of people in Taipei use public transport every day, and while many people owned scooters, not everyone had a car.

It is not a simple case of 'build it and they will come'. Good public transport requires investment in the right infrastructure and also the right communication platforms to inform people about what is in place. It also needs to be affordable for people to switch to public transport, while remaining commercially viable.

Taipei is not the only place to invest heavily in public transport infra-structure. China has experienced a boom in transport infrastructure. As people become more affluent, they want to travel around more. And as air pollution and carbon emissions increase, governments are realising that public transport is essential.

Even Canberra, where I live, is spending over $1 billion to build a light rail to connect the new northern suburb of Gungahlin to the city centre. The next phase would then connect the rail to the southern suburb of Woden. Canberra has traditionally lagged behind other cities and areas on public transport, so this is comparatively radical for a city of only 350,000 residents.

An article in *The Guardian* in early 2018 reported that Germany had announced it was considering making public transportation free in five major cities. The move is being considered as a way of reducing the number of private cars on the road, and to help Germany meet the European Union air pollution targets that it is struggling to meet, at the risk of big fines. The proposal will be tested in major cities including Bonn, Essen and Mannheim.

New technologies, including automated vehicles, will also change the way that public transport is built and operated. Watch this space—more disruption to come! In the meantime, taking a bus or train really is cheaper than driving a car, so it's wise to consider the proximity to public transport when you're choosing where to live.

FRUGALISTA CHALLENGE

Do you need your second car? Do you need a car at all? Are there some trips you could do by bicycle or even walking? Commit to walking, cycling or taking public transport at least once a week when you previously would have driven a car. Add up how much you'll save by leaving your car at home one day a week, using the lined pages at the back of this book if desired. Could you extend your challenge to more than one day a week? Or could you make it a permanent change?

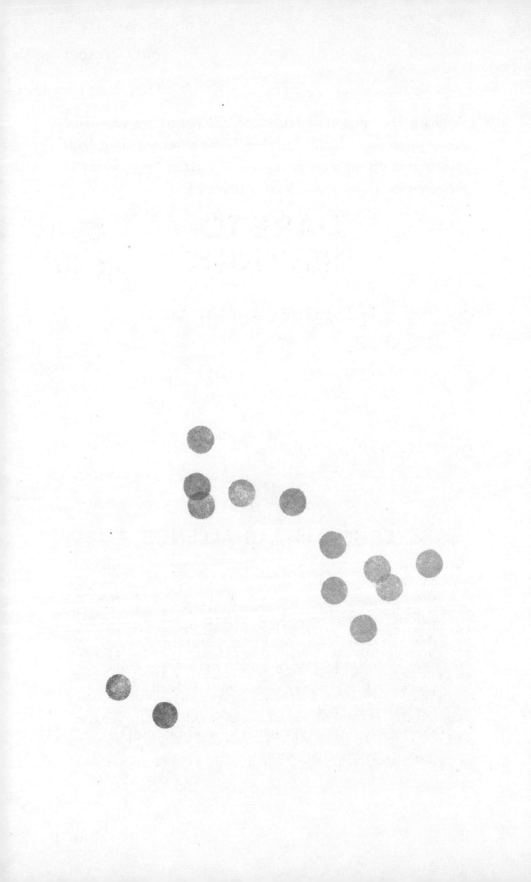

CHAPTER 7

DARE TO DISCOUNT

Never pay full price

DON'T BE AFRAID TO ASK

'You mean I can ask for a discount?' someone asked me recently when I shared how I got 12 per cent off my electricity bill. Yes, you most certainly can. And not just off your electricity bill.

I am always amazed at how *polite* we are here in Australia when it comes to spending money. Someone quotes a price, and we say, 'Oh, okay then' and hand over cash or a credit card. Maybe we have post-purchase dissonance afterwards, maybe we mutter and moan and complain inwardly, but rarely do we say anything if we think the price is too high. In fact, I have noticed that in Australia (compared with my friends in Taiwan and in Taiwanese and Chinese communities here), we rarely talk about money or prices or salaries or anything to do with our personal finances.

Since you're reading this book, you'll understand that I am a frugalista (and you are probably a frugalista yourself). So you'll forgive me for saying this: you are bloody stupid if you pay full price when you do not have to.

Of course, there are times when you cannot avoid paying full price or even where you choose to pay full price. I often bypass a doctor who bulk bills and pay full price if there is a particular doctor or health practitioner I want to see. I pay full price at the supermarket if I don't have time to go to ALDI or Costo, or if I want to shop at the farmers' markets. I go to an all-night pharmacy and pay full price if it is late at night and I need medication for one of my kids. I pay full price if I buy something on impulse or if I am in a rush. I pay full price if I am going to an event with family or work colleagues that I didn't organise, and over which I have no say about the price. I pay full price for clothing if there is something that I really like and that looks good on me. I pay full price if I get really good service at a shop and know that there will be good after-sales care. I pay full price for concert tickets if there is a band or performer I really want to see.

One of my blog readers made the point that she often pays full price to support her local community. Another friend once said that she felt sad that she didn't have coffee at her local cafe more often because the owners were lovely; sadly, it ended up closing down.

It is true that it's important to pay fair prices to support your local community, and it's important to support local businesses. However, you are not doing anyone a service if you buy things that are overpriced for the sake of it. In the long run, this won't help to build a sustainable community. I am surprised, though, at how many people consistently pay full price, especially when there are huge savings to be made. What is holding them back? I believe there are a few obstacles.

1. **Lack of time.** Scouting for deals involves time. Once you get in the habit, like me, comparing becomes part of the buying process. After a while, you know where to go to find the best deals. Sometimes people use brokers to help them find better deals. I use an insurance broker for this purpose, and after years of saying I would never use one,

I now use a mortgage broker, through whom I receive great deals on mortgages (more on this later). There are occasions, though, when you have to make a decision quickly and don't have the luxury of time. However, if you're already in the habit of looking for deals, you'll at least know where to go to buy things quickly and cheaply.

2. **Lack of interest.** Some people might find searching for deals boring, but not me. Neil and I find that it's fun to compare the best deals. We like to think of it as a challenge or competition. We love talking about where to get bargains, enjoy looking at different options and thinking outside the box. At the moment we are comparing prices on an overseas trip, tours for daytrips during a cruise and a new car (not until next year). We love thinking about and planning our travel — it's almost as much fun as being there.

3. **Lack of information.** The modern trading system is built on the notion that supply and demand are driven by adequate information. But in reality, consumers don't always have enough information to make a rational decision. We often buy products that are more expensive because we don't know where to shop to get the best deal.

In our internet age, this is becoming much less of an obstacle, but sometimes we don't have the information we need to make an informed decision. Or maybe we are scared to admit that we do not know enough about the subject matter. I certainly felt a little inadequate when I was thinking about which National Broadband Network (NBN) plan to choose.

My tip is to type the words 'site comparison' into a Google search. Say, for example, you are searching for perfume. Type 'Chanel No 5 site comparison' into your internet browser, and you will be given a range of options. If you have the luxury of time, you will find that over the next few days you will get pinged with ads for all sorts of perfumes—you might even end up with an even better deal than the current ones.

Comparing financial products is another area that can be a minefield. It isn't as simple as comparing apples with apples, as different products have different inclusions. Mortgages, for instance, can include things like redraws, offset accounts, linked credit cards and annual or monthly fees.

Another way to gather information is to ask—ask friends, neighbours, family members. Where did you buy your car? Which bank or credit union do you bank with? What is the rate on your mortgage? Are you happy with the service? What is the product like?

4. **Fear of the unknown.** I was talking to my mother recently about her mobile plan. I suggested a few cheaper options, but she chooses to remain with her current provider because the 'boys' there look after her. There is one young salesman in particular who is charming and who listens. She is unsure about technical things, and she feels safe with what she knows. It can be scary to move beyond your comfort zone. I am a bit like that when it comes to computers and cars. Many women are, which is why certain technical products are sold at a premium to women. For example, some mechanics bamboozle females and oversell products. The same happens to men: a man buying a present for his beloved in a jewellery shop (or perhaps even a lingerie store) is more likely to overspend.

5. **Habit.** So many people pay full price because they have always shopped at the same supermarket, banked at the same bank or gone to a shopping centre rather than shopping online. The world is changing and it is shaking up how we purchase things—the rise in e-commerce, including the arrival of Amazon Australia—is part of that. Major department stores will need to adapt or perish. It's time to

disrupt your own purchasing habits and think about whether you could shop in new or different ways.

6. **Fear of what other people think.** Would you go on a date with a man who used a voucher? I would. In fact, I would find that attractive. Who cares if you use a voucher at a restaurant? When I present a discount voucher, I often end up talking to the staff about the deals I get. I tell them how they can do the same. I find that many restaurant owners and staff regularly use vouchers to eat out at a discount.

And who cares if you have items in your supermarket trolley that are marked down because they're close to their 'best before' or 'use by' date? Maybe people are looking at you with envy at the good deals you got, rather than feeling sorry for you. Recently a friend posted on Facebook her shopping trolley filled with special deals. She was proud of her shopping bargains, and most of her friends were proud of her, too. I was envious and wanted to know which days to shop to get such good discounts.

Neil and I know of a couple who have a much lower income than us, but who insist on shopping at a more expensive supermarket. I think part of the problem is a misguided feeling that if you are doing it a bit tough, you don't want people to know. Perhaps you spend more than you can afford so you can feel wealthy. I don't understand that way of thinking, but I can understand that not having a lot of money is a sensitive issue for a lot of people.

My experience is that people are probably more likely to think negatively about you if you live an extravagant lifestyle that you flaunt, than if you show that you don't have much. You might feel like you are impressing people, but behind your back, they're wondering about the credit card debt you must be in or if you are running an illegal drug ring to finance your jet-setter lifestyle. This is the Australian tall poppy syndrome at work. We value authenticity.

7. **Brand loyalty.** Companies pay a fortune on marketing to build brand loyalty. In some cases, a particular brand is reliable and represents value. However, often a generic product will be just as good, if not better. Have you ever considered as you walk through a supermarket that cheaper products are often produced in the same factory as the well-known brands? When I was at high school we went on a tour of a pineapple processing factory. It was fascinating to watch workers place the same products in different tins, which carried different labels and were priced differently.

Supermarkets stock the same or very similar products in different packaging. Sometimes the address on the can or packet will give it away, although I have noticed a lot of generic brands try to keep it hidden. Where a generic product looks very close to the branded product in content, packaging, label and taste, it is likely that they are made in the same factory. If this wasn't the case, the brand name company would no doubt be suing the supermarket for stealing its brand.

It is similar when it comes to motor vehicles: sometimes cheaper Asian vehicles have components, such as motors, that are very similar to luxury European models, but for a lower price. Did you know that European luxury branded cars are not always built in Europe? According to an article that featured on motoring.com.au in July 2016, BMW has manufacturing plants in 14 countries including in South Africa, Mexico and China. Only some of its cars are still made in Germany.

I gave up brand loyalty a long time ago, and it seems I am not the only one. Ruslan Kogan, the founder of Kogan.com, was quoted in an article published in *INTHEBLACK* magazine as saying, 'There's a huge wave of change happening in the world, and people now care a lot more about the product than they do about the brand.' He started his multi-million-dollar business selling cheap televisions imported from China, so he knows a thing or two about how brand loyalty is becoming less important to consumers. He notes in particular that the growth of peer reviews means that consumers can easily judge quality and performance and are less likely to be swayed by the marketing of big name brands.

8. **Snobbery.** The snobbery factor is not the same as brand loyalty. Rather, it is about choosing to purchase a luxury brand so that other people will think you are cool or fashionable, or that you have lots of money. This snobbery factor is especially prevalent in the world of fashion.

There used to be a trend of wearing T-shirts that carried a luxury brand. Thankfully, that has largely stopped—I, for one, was never going to pay for free advertising for a fashion house. But there is still, for instance, a trend of buying an expensive handbag so that everyone will know you can afford one. Just because a handbag is Mimco or Prada or Coach doesn't mean it suits you, matches your clothes or is suitable for holding the things you need to carry around with you—even if it is authentic rather than counterfeit.

The same goes for clothing. Just because something is the latest fashion and carries a brand name, there's no guarantee you will look good in it.

9. **Shyness.** It can be scary to ask for a lower price, only to be turned down. This feeds into our fear of appearing cheap, poor or becoming ostracised from a particular social circle. 'You want a discount? You're dreaming!' But what do you have to lose? Maybe the answer will be no, but maybe it will be yes. You don't have to be aggressive or rude in asking for a discount—you will get the best deal by asking for it in a congenial manner.

HOW TO NEGOTIATE LIKE AN EXPERT

You don't have to be a professional negotiator handling multi-million-dollar deals to be good at negotiating. We use negotiation in many aspects of our life. If we're married or in a relationship with someone, we negotiate on a daily basis — how we spend money, where we go out for dinner, what movie we see, which friends we catch up with, where we go for Christmas. How successfully we negotiate determines how successful we are at getting what we want.

A lot of advice has been written about how to negotiate. Universities and business schools run courses on negotiating. There are books and expensive seminars. Salespeople immerse themselves in learning how to be persuasive. I don't claim to be an expert, but as a frugalista I do like a good deal. Here are my tips.

1. *Offer what the other side wants*

As a child, I used to love playing Monopoly. It became a consuming passion. I was never happy unless I won. While in most things I think I am rational and even nice, I take on a different persona when I play Monopoly. I become possessed.

I mustn't have been too egregious because my sister and other friends would still play with me even though I was intent on winning. Now that I am a mother, I play with my children and see that my youngest son has inherited the 'I like having lots of money and property' gene from me. He also throws spectacular tantrums when he doesn't win and lords it over us all when he does; as he is only six, we hope he grows out of it. But if he takes after me, perhaps he won't.

I don't wait for good luck when I play Monopoly: my secret weapon is to negotiate. I look around the board and work out what I want, who has it and what he or she might want in return. I identify that someone might want Trafalgar Square in exchange for Piccadilly, or that they are low on the money and could be coerced to give up their properties for cash. I've learnt that people don't like Old Kent Road or the railroads and tend to underrate them. The status of wanting to own Mayfair often makes people overextend, and I leverage this to my advantage.

Until recently I didn't think I had good negotiating skills, despite the fact that I had bought and sold properties. Looking back, I can see how playing Monopoly helped me to develop these skills.

In my professional life, I have a bit to do with international trade negotiators. It is a specialist discipline that requires technical knowledge and experience. However, similar to when playing Monopoly, a key issue is determining what the other side wants. When the stakes are big and there are multi-million (or even billion) dollar industries that want specific things, finding out and leveraging what the other side wants is an essential part of the negotiations. One technique is to negotiate the easy things first — this helps to build goodwill and rapport. It also provides an opportunity to glean what the sticking points are for the other side.

2. Build rapport

You are much more likely to want to do business or do a good deal with someone that you like. We tend to think about negotiating in terms of being shrewd, tough and aggressive — big, powerful, manly man stuff. But we are all human beings and like to feel good about the transactions we are involved in, not that we have been ripped off by an unscrupulous bastard.

When Neil and I are stickybeaking at properties together, we each play a different role. He looks through the property in detail. He notices things like shower screens that do not shut properly, wardrobes that need new door handles, cracks in walls that signal potential structural issues and the state of the plumbing. Neil is a technical officer, did the labouring when he built his own house and is meticulous in noticing structural details. He also reads the property inspection reports.

Meanwhile, you will find me chatting up the real estate agent.

Now to be clear, I am not flirting with the intent of forming a romantic relationship. Nor am I doing it with evil or insincere intent. I like real estate, and I like real estate agents. I often end up connecting with the agents on social media afterwards, and sometimes we do in fact become real friends and keep in contact. Often real estate agents are investors themselves. They got into the industry because they like property. They like talking about property and sharing their insights with investors. They have a wealth of information.

I like talking to the real estate agents at open homes because I like finding out more about the property, the area, the tenants, the potential for tenanting the property, what the estate agent likes about the property, what he or she doesn't like about the property, and how many other people are looking at it. Most of all, I want to find out why the vendors are selling.

Most people try to avoid the real estate agent when they visit an open house. They reluctantly provide their email address and they try to hide their true intentions and motivations. They think real estate agents are like bloodsucking mosquitoes on the hunt for commission (there is no getting around the fact that it is a commission-based industry). And when they do talk to real estate agents, they bluff and puff. 'Buyers are liars', an estate agent once said to me.

I break all the rules in the book about how you 'should' behave as a buyer. I am open, upfront and honest. I talk openly about my financial situation and what I am looking for, what else I am looking at and how I feel about a property. Most of all, I establish a rapport with the real estate agent based on trust.

When it comes to accepting offers, it isn't all about money. There were higher offers when my ex-husband and I purchased our first property, but we impressed as being sincere. When I worked as a law clerk, I would see offers on commercial property discarded because the sellers were concerned about the buyer's ability to cough up the dough. The agent wants his or her commission and wants to know that you are genuine in going through with the deal and won't mess them around.

The agent is the one who advocates for you. Just as you are assessing why someone is selling a property, they will assess your motivations for buying. You want the conversation between the agent and the vendor to go something like this: 'Although there is a higher offer from someone else, these people are genuine—they have bought before, they have finance approved and they are all set to go. It is a genuine offer and, while it is not the highest, I think you should take it.' On more than one occasion, a real estate agent has told me that there was a higher offer, but my offer was successful because I presented as being sincere.

As for the seller, parting with a property is often an emotional experience. If it is a family home, they may have grown up there and be reminiscing about running around the backyard with the sprinklers on or climbing the trees. They might have recently farewelled a parent, they might be selling as the result of the end of a relationship or they might be moving interstate. Or maybe they are a young couple who spent months or even years renovating the property together, choosing the right colour palette, painting walls, pulling out an old kitchen and choosing the new cupboards and appliances. Maybe it is purely an investment decision for the sellers, but I find that this is rare. The sellers will appreciate it if you are upfront and honest about your intentions, and if you act ethically. They will want to sell to you if you do the right thing by them.

3. Just ask — politely

Even though I am a frugalista, sometimes I am still a bit scared to ask for something at a lower price. It feels a bit embarrassing. It involves taking a risk, putting yourself out there by asking for something that is not automatically a given.

In Australia, most of the quoted prices are what we are conditioned to pay. However, just because we are quoted a price doesn't mean that we can't get a better deal.

Holly Maccue, who runs a successful coaching business for women, teaches something similar. I was privileged to participate in her 'Ask for what you want' five-day boot camp last year. During the boot camp, Holly talked about how she developed the courage to ask for what she wanted. It started with asking someone at a salad bar to serve her more of what she wanted: as her takeaway salad was being dished out, she saw it contained more cheap salad and not enough of the good stuff. So, she politely yet firmly asked for more — and she got it. What would you do? Would you accept that you were paying top dollar for iceberg lettuce, or would you have the courage to say, 'Could you please give me some more of the halloumi?'

Using words such as 'Is this your best price, please', or 'Could you please ask if there is any flexibility with the price', or 'Is this negotiable, please', or 'Could you do me a better deal, please' can get you a long way. My friend Mary Bernadette says that her trick is to ask in a firm but sweet voice, 'Is that the best price that you can do?' She did so well at negotiating on the phone that her boss used to come and listen in.

The magic words vary given the situation, but the golden word among them is 'please' — or at least a tone that is polite.

Sometimes you might be given a better deal by not asking. It happens to me occasionally, but not often. A blog reader told me that she sometimes gets a good deal by hesitating; by not agreeing to the price right away, a merchant might offer her a better price. But in general, I find that a business will not give you a discount unless you ask. Because usually, *if you don't ask, you don't get.*

Our modern-day commerce is based on the Ricardian principle of comparative advantage, which embraces the concept of open trade. The key principle is supply and demand, with the market setting the price based on rational information. By asking for a lower price, you are in effect being part of an efficient part of the open market process. If prices are always too high, a company will eventually go out of business. Likewise, if the prices are too low to meet overheads, it will go out of business unless it becomes more efficient. Your interaction is part of the process of sharing information, of testing the supply and demand process and giving companies information about the price that the customer is willing to pay.

Even when making a lower offer is openly discouraged, you might still have an opportunity to negotiate. I purchased an investment property in December 2017 and put in an offer that was $6000 lower than the advertised asking price. The price had already been dropped by $20,000.

At the time there was limited interest in purchasing in that area. We did not see another person at any of the open homes that we attended. I knew there had been two previous offers on that property that had fallen through, and that they were because of problems with the buyer rather than with the property. I factored this in when making my offer.

The real estate agent wouldn't accept it. 'The buyer will only consider offers at the full advertised price,' he said.

I persisted. 'I have presented a formal written offer. My partner and I are genuine buyers with good public service jobs, and our mortgage broker has said we would have no problems getting finance for this amount,' I said. 'I want you to put the offer to the owner.'

'I have been instructed not to present her with any offer below that amount,' he said.

I left it at that, but somewhat surprisingly, he did put the offer to the owner, and she did accept it. We were genuine buyers, and we now own the property.

The agent later told me that it turns out he could have sold the property at full value many times over, in part due to property prices starting to rise a month afterwards. We were lucky regarding timing — but was it really luck? Just like my experience of playing Monopoly, I believe in making my own luck.

We would have never secured this deal unless we asked. When you ask for a lower offer, a company can always say no, and in many circumstances they will. But not always. You'll never know unless you ask.

4. Loyalty pays

In Australian culture, we tend to shop around a bit for deals. But in Chinese culture, with which I am also familiar after living in China and Taiwan, people value the art of relationship building.

In Chinese, the term for relationship building is *guanxi*. It has a cultural meaning used in particular contexts, but in broad terms, when you have *guanxi* with someone, it means you have a reciprocal relationship with them. A *guanxi* relationship takes time to establish and is built on a strong foundation of trust and respect. If you have *guanxi* with someone, they will usually give you a discount, special deal or favour. It might be as small as giving you a few extra apples when you do your market shopping or treating you with extra respect.

Naturally, you are more likely to want to do business with someone whom you know and trust. You are more likely to want to sell something cheaply to someone who is a friend. For example, say you were selling your car. If a good friend, or someone you work with and know, approached you to buy it, you would be more likely to give him or her a good deal.

It can take time to build up *guanxi*, and it might not be feasible for certain transactions. But rather than running around and buying a lot of things from different stores chasing bargains, sometimes it can pay to consolidate and buy them all from the one store. A boutique owner might give you a bargain if you buy several outfits, for instance. Or perhaps you could leverage loyalty schemes that reward repeat business.

Airline frequent flyer schemes are an example of this, as are fashion brands that have special pre-season events offering their regular customers a discount. If you have multiple policies with the same utility provider, you might be able to 'bundle' to save money (although you should still negotiate the best deal and compare products).

WHEN EXPERTS CAN HELP

Being a proud frugalista, I like to do things myself. However, it takes time to research many deals. As a mother of two young children who works full-time and is in a new marriage, blogs, writes and is active in her community, sometimes I don't have as much time to research deals as I would like. For time-poor people like me, the services of an expert can help.

An expert can save you money because they know where to get the best deals and have established relationships with providers, and they also offer quality service. They can bargain effectively because they have the power of quantity. They also do it every day, so they understand the market that they are in, including common pitfalls. They know which providers are good and which ones to stay away from.

Last year, for the first time, I decided to use an insurance broker. I always thought I had good insurance deals. Because I had several insurance policies with the same provider, I was being offered a discount across all of them. I honestly thought I had the best deal—I had even negotiated a small discount.

Then I met an insurance broker at a networking function and got chatting. 'So, do you specialise in commercial insurance broking?' I asked. At that stage, that's what I thought insurance brokers did: I didn't think they would offer insurance for the average person like me.

'No, we do insurance broking for anyone who requires it,' she said. 'If you think about it, you probably need several insurance policies—home and contents, car insurance (maybe for more than one car) and, in your case, landlord insurance.' She was right. I did, in fact, need six different insurance policies.

Being curious, I wanted to know why anyone would need a broker for insurance.

'Well, for one, if you need to claim on an insurance policy, the insurance company is much more likely to treat your claim as a priority,' she said. 'They know that if they stuff you around, we would not recommend them to any of our clients in the future. They value our repeat business, so the companies we use all give our clients preferential treatment.'

Our friends Geoff and Jan had to wait several months for someone from an insurance company to come and examine their claim. The roof of their house had blown off in a freak storm, and their home had suffered extensive damage. Because the issue was isolated to a few homes in their rural area, the insurance company did not realise how serious it was. Geoff and Jan had to wait three months just before their claim could be assessed.

Having my case fast-tracked in the unlikely event I needed to claim on insurance seemed like a good option to me.

But that's not all. It turns out that a common problem with insurance policies is that by having multiple separate policies, you are charged for personal indemnity insurance for every policy. You can reduce your premium by consolidating into one policy, easily done through a broker.

Another common problem I discovered is that people are routinely underinsured. I honestly had no idea what a typical amount of insurance was, and what was fair and reasonable to ask for. How much would I need if I had to replace everything I owned? It turned out my landlord insurance did not include contents insurance, even though if there was a fire in an apartment I would need to replace chattels inside, such as curtains and kitchen cupboards.

I also discovered that I was paying a much higher premium on landlord insurance to be covered for loss of rent on properties. As my properties were all rented to quality tenants who were regularly paying, I had a good property manager and the rental vacancy rate was low, this insurance was probably not necessary. I appreciated being given different quotes that allowed me to see in detail what the difference was so that I could make an informed decision, weighing the costs against the risk.

Overall, by using an agent, I saved around $300 per year. I felt surprised because I thought I already had competitive policies. But more important than the saving, using a broker ensured I had the appropriate level of insurance. It hardly took me any time at all as my broker did all the legwork, and she even arranged for the refund from the previous providers.

Last year, for the first time, I also used a mortgage broker. I had always avoided using a mortgage broker. I prided myself on my ability to do my own research and fill out my own forms. But then I found a good price online, and when I investigated, I discovered it was offered through a mortgage broker.

The first time I spoke with my broker at Mortgage House I was sceptical. I told him that I had chosen a cheap online product previously and that the service had been bad. 'I feel like I sold my soul to the devil in exchange for a low rate,' I told him.

'I am not like that,' he promised. 'I will guide you through the loan application process, and then you will have dedicated customer support after the loan settles.'

He was right. He was extremely patient and helpful, and went out of his way to expedite my application. He was able to offer me a rate that was 0.4 per cent lower than comparable rates, with no fees or charges. His service was so good that Neil and I went with the same brokerage company when we purchased another two properties a few months later.

Not all brokers are the same. Many charge 'trailing commissions', which means that they receive a small commission for the lifetime of the loan. The commission structure provides them with an incentive to only offer certain products to you, even though there might be cheaper options available.

The key is to ask questions of your broker, including where his or her fees come from. It also pays to double check and do your own research, especially with big-ticket items such as mortgages. Mortgage products can change over time, and what is a good product in 2019 might no longer be as competitive in 2024. It is important to review your mortgage and other details periodically so that you have the best deal.

FRUGALISTA CHALLENGE

Ask for a better deal on something or get someone else to negotiate a better deal for you. How much can you save? $50? $100? $1000? Or even more.

CHAPTER 8

FINDING DEALS

Coupons, vouchers, daily deals and more

THE COUPON CULTURE

In the United States, money bloggers and influencers spend a lot of time talking about coupons. What are they and do they make any difference? Why don't we use them in Australia?

In *The Millionaire Next Door: The Surprising Secrets of America's Wealthy*, authors Thomas J. Stanley and William D. Danko relate several stories about multi-millionaires. In one story, a husband tells his wife that he has given her USD$8 million worth of stock that he had just taken to market. (This was over 20 years ago, so the value would probably be more like USD$12.5 million today.) The wife smiled and said, 'I appreciate this, I really do.' Then she went back to clipping 25c- and 50c-off food coupons from the newspapers. 'Nothing is so important as to interrupt her Saturday-morning chores,' concluded the authors.

The story was related in the context of discussing how many of the super-rich in the United States were inherently frugal—and their spouses even more so. I loved the idea that a multi-millionaire was still looking to use 25c- and 50c-off coupons; she understood that every dollar counts and that big savings start with small habits.

Fast forward 20 years, and couponing in the United States is bigger than ever. It has not yet caught on in the same way in Australia (with some exceptions that I will detail below), but I predict that it is about to take off big time. Get your scissors ready!

I was recently out to dinner with some fabulous frugalista female friends. One of my friends was telling me that there are whole television shows devoted to showing how American women snip coupons and then go out shopping with them. Apparently there is a real art to the coupon-snipping habit. There are even groups of women who snip coupons together as a social savings activity.

This prompted me to watch an episode of *Extreme Couponing*. In the episode I watched (Season 1, Episode 2—yes there is more than one season, and it is very popular), two women demonstrated how to coupon like a professional (they saw it as akin to a full-time job). Rebecca Routson described couponing as her 'talent' and proudly told everyone, 'I wake up thinking about coupons all the time. Sometimes I get so excited I can't fall asleep because I know it is such a good deal.'

Couponing can be addictive and obsessive. Rebecca's store included 42 rolls of paper towel and enough potato chips to feed 800 people.

During the show she joked to her boyfriend, 'I'm going to punch you on camera,' when he interfered with her method of neatly stacking jars in her trolley. At the checkout, they needed to call five friends to help them as there was a limit of only one special coupon per customer. In all, they spent five hours at the supermarket.

Jessica Hacker also had a stockpile—in her case, the couponing mini supermarket at her home had around $20,000 worth of items that only cost her $2000 to purchase. This included 75 boxes of cereal and enough dishwashing powder and tablets to wash 450 loads of dishes. 'I think my stockpile is almost as beautiful as my family', she gushed as she talked about how she loves showing off her carefully organised stockpile area. She plans her monthly food menu carefully to take advantage of specials and to use up the stockpile.

It is easy to be critical of the time that these women spend on couponing, but it clearly makes a difference. Jessica talked about how the recession had hurt her family; she is a stay-at-home mum, and her husband is a tradie whose work had been negatively impacted by the Global Financial Crisis. Couponing is a way for them to live affordably, and she views it as her job. Their total monthly budget for food is only USD$160, made possible through couponing.

Do the savings make it worthwhile? In the episode I watched, Rebecca purchased USD$562.81 worth of groceries and paid only USD$25.91, a 96 per cent saving. Jessica saved even more, purchasing USD$680 worth of groceries for only USD$6.46, a 99 per cent saving.

There are certainly some great bargains if you are disciplined and organised. But as I watched, I noticed a few issues.

Firstly, most of the coupon specials are for processed foods — chips, tomato pasta sauce, hot dogs, cheese snacks, breakfast cereals, etc. A diet like this is not healthy or sustainable in the long term, although I would be lying if I said I never ate potato chips or hot dogs. The show demonstrated that it is possible to eat healthily with couponing, but you would arguably eat a better diet if you used fresh ingredients and cooked from scratch.

Secondly, to coupon effectively you need to purchase things when they are on special and then stockpile. Stockpiling requires space. In my inner-city apartment with my husband and kids (where I also rent out a room), space is at a premium. The space underneath my bed is full, and my wardrobe is bulging. I don't have excess space to use for stockpiling, and it's worth considering the extra costs of doing it — if you could earn up to $100 a night with an Airbnb, is stockpiling this food effective? If you had a large garage or big cupboards, it would be easier to do.

Thirdly, the coupon culture leads to people buying things they want rather than need. Who can resist a bargain? Not me. I would be a sucker for buying up excess items because I had a coupon. And that's the point — retailers and marketing departments want you to spend up big on products you might not otherwise choose. This includes processed foods, vitamin supplements and fad foods.

Supermarkets and other companies certainly gain from couponing. They do it because it allows them to promote new items, draw people into supermarkets and elicit marketing information from consumers, among other things. Perhaps they don't intend for people to use coupons as aggressively as some people do, but there is no law against doing so.

COUPONING OUTSIDE OF THE UNITED STATES

We don't really have a couponing culture in Australia — yet. Or at least, not one that we identify as a coupon culture. I feel certain that the coupon culture is coming to other countries. That's because technology makes coupons easier to use, scan and redeem at the checkout or counter rather than needing to cut out coupons.

Couponing also includes innovative apps, such as the Hungry Jack's 'Shake & Win' app. I bet most of the users of the app (predominantly young males) don't see it as a coupon. The idea is that you shake your mobile phone for an opportunity to win something free or discounted at Hungry Jack's. The app provides the location of the nearest Hungry Jack's store, and you can redeem the deal as long as you arrive within 20 minutes. The app quickly gained popularity when it was released in Australia in 2012.

Neil recently found a Domino's Pizza 'mega-savings coupon' in the letterbox. The coupon was active for ten days. Although you didn't need to cut out and present the coupon, you did need to quote the discount code to redeem it. Once again, many Australians might not think of this as 'couponing' in the *Extreme Couponing* sense, but it is still effectively a coupon.

In this chapter, I want to look at some of the ways you can purchase good-quality deals using coupon-style products so that you can get an item, service or experience at less than full price. Although we don't yet have as many 'clip out and scan' deals as they do in the United States, we do already have a lot of 'specials' in brochures, discount books and apps. I believe they are coupons—just marketed differently.

Brochures

Firstly, I want to make the point that you only save money if you buy something that is a need rather than a want. If you are only buying something because it is on special, and if it is something you won't use or don't really need, then it is not a special at all. A good example of this is buying more fruit and vegetables than you need and then having to throw items out after a few weeks (I am guilty of this). This actually creates more work.

The best saving is not to spend money on stuff that will clutter up your life. However, if there are certain things you need (or really, really want—let's face it, we all indulge in occasional luxuries), using brochures wisely to identify specials can be a great way to go.

Most supermarkets and retailers put out brochures advertising specials. Unless you have a 'no junk mail' sticker on your mailbox, you will probably receive a lot of them. If you opt out of receiving brochures by mail, you can receive most online. I subscribe to the weekly ALDI brochure and I also receive regular coupon special offers from Costco. I don't mind reading the BIG W catalogue, I love the styling at Kmart, and I shop regularly at Chemist Warehouse so I always scan their special bargains (I sometimes stock up on kids' presents ahead of unexpected birthday parties). I don't read brochures religiously the same way some people in the US clip coupons. But at key times like 'end of financial year' sales, mid-year toy sales, or in the lead-up to Christmas, I find that reading and comparing the specials saves me a packet (and a lot of time traipsing around).

If you want to view a consolidated list of Australian brochures, you can find them online at salefinder.com.au. SaleFinder is a useful tool for seeing sales across several merchants. It also enables you to identify specials you might not otherwise have information about.

Most of the specials in brochures are extremely good deals — in fact, retailers often sell them at below cost price. These items are termed 'loss leaders' in the retail industry. The idea is that the supermarket or department store will sell some items as an incredible special deal to lure shoppers into the store. Sometimes the store will carry the loss, but often the suppliers or manufacturers financially support the special deal in exchange for prominence on the shelf. Regardless of who is paying for them, these are often genuine offers at genuinely low prices.

The best offers are pictured on the front and back of brochures. The most attractive items must catch your eye to be effective to the retailer as a marketing tool. A good front page encourages you to flick through the brochure, and go to the store to buy the item (and others). I've found that certain items tend to be in the brochures on a semi-regular basis, so if you're patient you can stock up on bargains. I buy 10 kilogram bags of rice when they are on special.

Have you ever seen a special advertised as only allowing a 'maximum spend'? You might think that this is designed to limit commercial businesses or others from buying up all the specials. However, it's usually designed to encourage you to buy more than one item by planting the idea that you need to buy the three or four that you're allowed. It's a psychological tool used by retailers that can be effective.

There are real savings to be made in buying 'loss leader' special items. The trick is obviously to only buy items on special if you need them, and to avoid stockpiling too much just because they're cheap. You also need to be organised to buy the specials before they expire or sell out. Some stores will still offer you the deal afterwards, but not all will.

Costco

Costco specials are termed 'coupons', and their brochure is designed to look like a pile of coupons. You don't need to present a coupon for the deal to be effective — it happens automatically at the checkout. They are always generous discounts off already in-stock items. On recent trips, I have bought packaged croissants, my favourite prosecco label and Huggies nappies (a gift for Neil's niece and her husband who had a second child).

In the lead-up to our wedding, I kept an eye out for Costco coupons for things that we would use at the reception, such as specials on prosecco or other alcohol or bulk catering supplies. If those items came up, we pounced.

ALDI

ALDI specials are for items that are only in store for a short period (e.g. ski jackets), as opposed to Costco specials, which are reductions on everyday items. ALDI is famous for its Special Buys, where items come in on a particular day and are only available until sold out. Certain items sell out quickly, including a rocking chair that apparently sold out in just minutes. It looked good — I remember seeing it in the brochure and thinking that although I had no space for it, I still really wanted one.

And that's the magic of ALDI Special Buys—they draw you in. I remember spending one Boxing Day queuing up at ALDI for an advertised special. There was a whole group of people positioning their trolleys, which reminded me of a Formula 1 race (or dodgem cars). There can be huge savings on ALDI Special Buys, so the queuing up and rushing into the store is worth it for particular items.

ALDI's annual winter snow sale, held in Australia in May, is its biggest day of the year, according to news.com.au. ALDI sells items such as waterproof snow jackets, gloves, goggles and thermals much cheaper than other snow and skiing retail outlets. When I say cheaper, I am talking about jackets that cost around $70 as opposed to several hundred dollars, and goggles for $20 rather than $100. When I took my kids skiing last year, it was easy to lose them on the snowfields as they were engulfed in a sea of skiing kidlets who looked just like them in their ALDI harlequin-patterned jackets. I remember once reading an article about how ALDI's snow sale means that skiing is no longer a sport exclusively for the rich.

It is hard NOT to read an ALDI brochure. It has good pictures and prices, and it pitches products at the aspirational middle class. I want to live the lifestyle of the people in the brochures — I want to be part of that happy, skiing, tennis-playing, fashionable, healthy, got-it-all-together family who sit down to an ALDI roast at the end of the week.

The brochures are stacked everywhere in the store, including along the checkout so you can read while you're waiting, and checkout staff will always ask you if you would like a brochure when you pay. There are more piles of brochures in the bagging area. But if you do miss out, you can subscribe to receive the brochure via email, like I do, so there is no excuse for ever missing a bargain — especially not the big snow sale.

A good friend of mine, and a frugalista champion, routinely avoids the middle aisles of ALDI, instead skirting around the edges and only buying food and grocery items. The inner aisles are full of Special Buys items, all carefully themed. It's hard not to find a bargain. I am less disciplined than her. On a recent trip, I came away with a black skirt for work and pondered over plants and kitchen items. And I have often been conned into buying books or toys for my boys.

Tourist magazines

On a recent work trip to Melbourne, I opened a glossy tourist magazine in my hotel room. Inside I noticed many 'coupons' for tourist attractions that you could tear out and present. Do they work? Absolutely. If you are planning on buying opals or visiting a tourist attraction or theme park, they do deliver a discount. Don't dismiss these just because they look junky, or because they are just for touristy places (sometimes you might want to shop and explore like a tourist). Accept that they are geared to tourists, not to well-educated locals who would have the benefit of time in which to shop around. But like everything, don't just accept the discounts at face value. Do a quick internet search or ask around and you might find a better deal. Also note whether they include any requirements to spend money before you can claim a discount.

VOUCHERS

Vouchers were traditionally … vouchers—bits of paper that you took to a store or restaurant that entitled you to a discount. You usually presented them at the counter when you bought something. For example, you would purchase a meal and then, when you went to pay, you would present a 'buy one, get one free' voucher, which entitled you to pay for one meal and get a meal of similar value for free.

Vouchers were a novelty when they first came onto the scene. These days many of them have gone high tech; vouchers are on websites, emails and also on special apps. The range and quality of voucher items have improved dramatically. Vouchers are now a competitive field, with some players vying with each other for bargains.

Shop A Docket

One of the earliest vouchers was the Shop A Docket system, which printed special deals on the back of supermarket dockets. Shop A Docket has been in the Australian market for 30 years and yes, it still exists. I remember when specials first started appearing on the back of dockets. It was so exciting to discover something that was cheap or even free — revolutionary in fact. I loved scanning the back of receipts, and I loved keeping them.

Over time I became a bit blasé about Shop A Docket deals. I guess part of the problem was they weren't always for deals that interested me. As a teenager, I wasn't looking to have carpet steam cleaned, or for pensioner-style one-for-one meals. However, some of the deals are extremely good; my close friend enjoyed a luxury cruise for half price using a Shop A Docket special.

Shop A Docket still prints deals on the back of receipts, but you don't have to wait for these vouchers. You can search online for deals and print them off, and you can also download their app. I found there was not much on the website, but there were more deals on the app. Their cruise deals are especially good, and there are some great local restaurant deals from time to time.

The Entertainment Book

Often nicknamed 'the gold book', this book was traditionally filled with vouchers available for most major cities in Australia. Entertainment Book memberships now include a digital membership option, which works via a mobile phone app.

The Entertainment Book is only sold through charities or social organisations, which use it for fundraising. An organisation receives 20 per cent of the purchase price of each book, so in Canberra this equates to $12 from the sale of each $60 book.

Being curious about the business model, I asked my Entertainment Book sales rep how the company makes money. He explained that participating businesses provide their deals for free in return for receiving advertising benefits (and for many, there is also a desire to help their local community). The company behind the Entertainment Book makes money from the sale of books and memberships.

There are thousands of deals in the book that are available year-round. The Canberra book claims that it has $20,000 worth of discounts. Entertainment Book members also receive email alerts about special deals from time to time and are eligible to enter competitions.

NRMA membership benefits

If you are a member of the National Roads and Motorists' Association (aka NRMA), similar motoring associations or a customer of certain utility providers, you might have access to a set of membership benefits. Traditionally, these were in a book but now many are online.

The NRMA membership scheme includes reduced prices on car hire and visits to theme parks. I find these membership benefits are not as extensive as the Entertainment Book, but the advantage is that they come free with your membership. Some frugalistas find that these are enough for their needs and choose to use just these benefits, without purchasing an Entertainment Book.

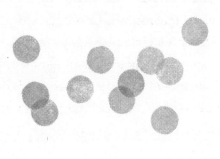

HOW I SAVED OVER $600 A YEAR USING MY ENTERTAINMENT BOOK MEMBERSHIP

Years ago, a good friend used to go out of her way to try to convince me to buy an Entertainment Book from her. I was polite but firm. 'No, thank you,' I said. 'I wouldn't use it.'

At the time it was probably true, as my ex-husband and I were living an extremely frugal existence while we built up our property investments. We did not go out much, preferring to dine in rather than eat out. We did not even go out to movies often, nor shows, and we rarely went on holidays. I also didn't stop to investigate how the Entertainment Books worked. I had seen the vouchers used in fast food outlets, but that was pretty much it. The top restaurants in the 'gold' section were foreign to me, like something from another world. In any case, Canberra's food scene in those days was not as exciting as it is now.

Fast forward to three years ago, when I decided to become involved in my work's family network. The lady who sold the Entertainment Books to raise funds for the network was going overseas with work, so she asked me to go to the launch and then help her sell the books.

I attended the launch, picked up promotional materials and flicked through a copy of the book. I could not help but wonder: were these books just a marketing con designed to extort soft-hearted do-gooders who wanted to support a charity? Were they only useful for people who ate out a lot? Or was there actually something in them?

That night I sat down and went through the book in detail, cataloguing how I could use my membership to save money. While still definitely on the frugal spectrum, I found that there were many ways in which I could make savings. I felt quite excited, actually, and filled with a sense of the possibility of what I could achieve.

This year marks the fourth time that I have used an Entertainment Book membership. The principal areas in which I save are the gift cards, especially the WISH eGift Cards. These allow Entertainment Book members to shop at Woolworths, BIG W, Dan Murphy's and BWS at a five per cent discount. I also use discounted gift cards at JB Hi-Fi for birthday gifts. Because my family is spread throughout Australia, I send flowers for significant events—the Petals special deal enables me to get 20 per cent off.

While I love cooking at home, Neil and I enjoy dining out from time to time. We are walking distance from three main restaurant precincts, including Canberra's hipster Lonsdale Street cafe strip. Several quality restaurants in the area offer good Entertainment Book discounts, most around 25 per cent off. I don't think I eat out much compared to many people, but over the course of the year we redeemed nine restaurant vouchers.

My philosophy is to buy the book and support my local

charity, and if I redeem deals for two quality meals out over the course of the year (e.g. an anniversary or birthday) I will easily get my money back. I don't worry about trying to use up each and every deal in the book—I've never heard of anyone being able to do that, and on average people seem to save a few hundred dollars.

The biggest reason I find that people don't make use of the book is that they are too scared to redeem vouchers because they don't want to look cheap. This is a perception issue rather than a reflection of the substance of what is in the book.

Last year I saved around $640. I'm sure I have forgotten something, even with my app helping me remember what I have redeemed vouchers for. The biggest savings were on accommodation and WISH eGift cards. We use the eGift cards when shopping at Woolworths, BIG W, Dan Murphy's, and when filling up at certain Caltex/Woolworths petrol stations. The table opposite shows how I saved money.

Item	Saving
WISH eGift cards, $1000 @ 5% discount	$50
JB Hi-Fi gift cards, $200 @ 5% discount	$10
Accommodation — Pier One Sydney, one night (attending a blogging award with my mum)	$70
Accommodation — Lake Crackenback, three nights (annual skiing holiday with my dad and Neil)	$210
Chemist Warehouse — $10 for purchases over $50	$30
Virgin Australia — 5% off when purchasing gift vouchers	$30
Petals flower delivery — 20% off	$40
Restaurants/dining out (including McDonald's and Subway)	$200
Total savings	**$640**

GROUP BUYING SITES

Have you ever bought a voucher from a website that enables you to eat out at a restaurant at a discount? If so, you are participating in a multi-billion-dollar growth industry called group buying.

With group buying, you purchase in advance from a specialist coupon or daily deal company. The company then gives you a voucher to print off and present when you redeem the service you need. If you are planning on going on a holiday or out to dinner sometime, the idea is that you purchase now when the item is on special, then use the voucher when you need it. Most of the deals are advertised online; increasingly, the deals are available via apps.

For example, you might pay $50 for a restaurant meal for two that is worth $100. You purchase the voucher online on Monday from a company such as Groupon. You then make a booking with the restaurant for that Saturday. On Saturday, you order and enjoy the meal, and then you present the voucher at the end of the meal instead of paying. You might need to pay extra if you order more food or drinks, but the idea is that you have prepaid for a special deal.

I have used several of these vouchers. I always read the fine print carefully as there are often restrictions around when the voucher can be redeemed and the type of food you can order. It is important to communicate up front with the restaurant or provider so that the staff know what you are redeeming. One restaurant I visited had certain items that it did not include — there was an expensive main meal roast item that was treated differently. If you know what is included and what is excluded, you can order around it.

How do group buying websites work? The coupon company agrees to promote the services of certain businesses on the condition that they provide large discounts to the consumers. A key issue here is that the service or product is not provided by the person selling you the voucher, which can be a problem in the event that one of the customers goes out of business. Further, there can be issues with meeting all the conditions (e.g. it usually must be used by a particular time, which can be difficult to lock in if a restaurant suddenly becomes busy and you can't get a reservation before the voucher expires).

On its website, Fair Trading New South Wales warns about some of the risks of group buying. It cautions that it 'has received an increasing number of enquiries and complaints about group buying, particularly in areas such as hair, beauty and personal care services, restaurants and cleaning services. Common complaints include non-supply and incomplete supply of goods or services, and difficulty in booking services and redeeming vouchers.'

You can mitigate the risks by following the tips that Fair Trading provides, namely you should:

1. Make sure you are aware of exactly what goods and services you are paying for, and what isn't included in the deal.

2. Carefully check all of the terms and conditions of sales, especially the expiry dates on vouchers.

3. Check with the website you are purchasing from to see if they offer refunds in the event that the company providing the service goes out of business before you have a chance to redeem the vouchers.

4. Understand that there can be delays in making bookings for vouchers purchased through group sales, as they can create a high demand.

Some of the larger companies operating group buying sites are explored in the following pages.

FIRST TABLE

You dine for only 50 per cent when you book an early bird special through First Table. By paying $10 to book a participating restaurant for a table of two or four, you are entitled to 50 per cent off the price of the food bill (drinks excluded). Unlike many other deals, you pay the restaurant after you have dined (but you pay for the voucher up-front). The catch is that you must arrive on time and not linger. The restaurant does not have to honour your voucher (even though you have paid for it) if you are more than 15 minutes late for your booking.

People eat early for all sorts of reasons: before seeing a movie or show, straight after work, or because they get up early and go to bed early. And if you are inclined to eat at a restaurant early, why not save money on your meal?

Early bird deals are not new. I have seen restaurants offer early bird specials from time to time, and while they are a good idea to help restaurants get people in for an early sitting, it somehow feels kind of desperate when restaurants advertise for this, like they can't get enough bookings to fill the restaurant. Many years ago, I saw a billboard advertising early bird specials outside a restaurant and I made the mistaken assumption that the restaurant (which is still going strong) was struggling. Would you go into a restaurant you didn't know if it was empty? Giving discounts to help drum up business earlier in the night makes good business sense as it helps the restaurant look vibrant, which will hopefully attract new customers.

First Table has operated in New Zealand and major Australian cities for some time. At the time of writing, it had just rolled out to Canberra. A blog reader said that she uses it regularly in London and finds it useful. I expect to hear more about First Table, and copycat companies, as more people become aware of the benefits of dining early.

MY EXPERIENCE OF FIRST TABLE

It's 5.25 pm and we are peddling furiously on our bikes. The reason? We have a 5.30 pm reservation at a Korean restaurant and we do not want to be late. Neil likes to be on time or early. I struggle a bit, but don't like to be too late. In this case, we cannot be late because we have a First Table reservation.

I paid $5 for our First Table voucher using a special introductory rate (and I also got $5 off my next voucher by sharing my reservation on Facebook). We are entitled to 50 per cent off our food bill, but it can be voided if we are more than 15 minutes late. Since our apartment is close to the city, we thought it would be quickest to cycle rather than drive (and park) or walk—thus the furious cycling.

We were happy to dine early; in fact, we planned for it as we were attending an event at 6.30 pm and wanted to eat beforehand. Our conditions stated that we had to arrive by 5.30 pm and vacate by 7.30 pm.

We arrived at the restaurant around 5 minutes late. Well, more like 10 minutes, but within the 15-minute time frame. There were several other people at the restaurant already. 'Are they also on First Table deals?' I wondered.

The wait staff knew of our booking and led us to a table with 'reserved' marked on it. I explained we couldn't stay for long, and so we ordered quickly. I thought we might have had a restricted or separate menu, but no, we could order anything.

We ordered rump steak, pork shoulder and chicken drumsticks for the Korean barbecue, served with rice and lettuce. We washed it down with jujube tea for me and a pear cider for Neil. We enjoyed our meal.

I looked around and felt almost smug. The restaurant was a third full and we were all eating the same food, enjoying the same experience, but we were getting 50 per cent off the bill.

When it came time to pay, it was cheap but not super-cheap. When you take into account the $10 booking fee ($5 in our case) and the fact that drinks are not included, it was around par with using the Entertainment Book (this restaurant was listed in there as well). On the basis of our calculations (below), we were $4 better off with this voucher (on the basis of using a discounted voucher that cost only $5). It would be more valuable if we were in a group of four and planning for a bigger meal. But for me, I am not really up for a big, heavy, multi-course meal at 5.30 pm (or any time).

Regular price
Food: $48.00
Drinks: $13.50
Total: $61.50

First Table
Food: $24.00
Drinks: $13.50
Voucher: $10.00
(I only paid $5.00)
Total: $47.50
(or $42.50 with the discounted voucher)

Entertainment Book
Food and drinks: $61.50
Discount (25% off total bill): $15.38
Total: $46.12

'What is your experience of using First Table?' I asked our waitress when we paid.

'It is generally good,' she said. 'We are busier later, in any case, so this allows us to get people in before the rush. Actually, I use First Table myself when I go out. There are some really good restaurants that take part in the scheme.'

Most of the Canberra restaurants I previewed on First Table when making my booking had start times of between 5.00 pm and 6.00 pm. One was a bar that had weekend specials at 8.30 pm. A 6.00 pm start for a 7.30 to 8.00 pm finish is reasonable. I was once taken to a swanky and somewhat pretentious restaurant and it was so hard to get reservations that we had to dine at 6.00 pm anyway. Why not get a discount for doing so?

Would I use First Table again? Yes, but next time I'd book for a group of four people (with friends who are likely to be on time!).

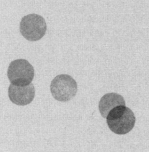

CUDO (PREVIOUSLY LIVING SOCIAL)

A friend at work recommended Living Social to me when I wanted to get a massage, as her favourite Thai massage place was often featured.It was an extremely good deal and allowed me to have a 90 minute pamper for around what I would normally pay for 45 minutes.

Living Social, now owned by Groupon and renamed Cudo, has a range of short-term specials on restaurants, experiences and travel. Some of the luxury travel is pretty swishy. I had to unsubscribe from the daily email alerts because I found myself daydreaming of exotic luxury holidays and it was getting a bit distracting at work.

The offers in Canberra are few but exceptionally good value. I have had three cost-effective meals courtesy of Cudo, including a group meal for three couples. I find merchants are often keen to match the deal without the voucher. Twice businesses have offered me the same or similar deal when I inquire about or present the voucher. They have done this at their own initiative—I haven't tried to undermine the Cudo system. I don't understand the pricing system, but I suspect businesses pay Cudo a fee every time a deal is redeemed. Accordingly, once they have made contact with you, some businesses will be keen to have you back again at a lower price than that offered to the general public if you inquire politely.

SPREETS

Spreets is an Australian-founded company that, according to *Business Insider Australia*, was sold to Yahoo for $40 million in 2011.

I had never heard of Spreets before one of my readers mentioned that she uses it. However, now that I know about it, I will be visiting it again because it pulls together many of the best deals across several sites, including Cudo, Scoopon and Groupon. It is, in essence, an amalgam of different deals and functions a bit like a comparison site.

FINDER

Like Spreets, Finder provides an amalgam of other deals. Finder is a heavily promoted website that aims to offer the best deals on a range of financial and consumer products. It is promoted through ads on television and high-profile advertising at major sports events. Whenever a company spends big on advertising, I am immediately suspicious about how it can afford to do so. Maybe I just have a suspicious mind. I prefer to do my own research when time permits, but I do find this a useful site to use for baseline comparisons.

Searches for coupons in Australia will direct you to Finder. When I clicked on some special coupons advertised, I found that many were not really coupons in the true sense—more like advertised specials. For example, Chemist Warehouse, where I regularly shop, had a 50 per cent off coupon, but really it was their guarantee to cut the cost of most prescriptions by 50 per cent. There may be some bargains on here, but I don't find it as useful as Spreets.

SCOOPON

Scoopon was founded in an Australian garage in 2010. Its best-known sister is Catch of the Day. Although I have bought from Catch of the Day, Scoopon doesn't operate in Canberra, so I haven't used it. However, I might use a voucher when visiting family in Melbourne or the Gold Coast. Scoopon lists some restaurants, but its strength is accommodation and travel deals.

GROUPON

Groupon has been in Australia since 2011, but it is far from being a newcomer to the world of coupon savings. Its website claims that, within Australia, it has a customer base of 5 million people, who have purchased

15 million vouchers. Globally, the Groupon app has been downloaded more than 139 million times.

Originally launched in Chicago, Groupon was a stock market hit when it first launched but then did not take off as quickly as expected because of copycats and other contenders. However, it is fighting back: for instance, Groupon bought Living Social (now Cudo) in 2016, and its future has been looking up since actress Tiffany Hadish told Jimmy Kimmel about the time she took Will Smith and wife Jada Pinkett Smith on an alligator swamp tour using a Groupon voucher. (Will and Jada didn't know what a Groupon was—they thought she had a private group booking for a boat.)

Groupon's interface is very slick, and the app is extremely easy to use. It has a solid selection of special deals—even for Canberra. Groupon is my new go-to app for deals when travelling interstate or even overseas, especially as it has a good function for navigating deals that are nearby.

TRAVELZOO

I am surprised that more people don't know about Travelzoo. Perhaps it's because Travelzoo is based in the United States, but this company is massive. Its website claims that it has more than 28 million members in North America, Europe and Asia Pacific. It lists deals from more than 2000 providers, and has a team of experts who review deals. Travelzoo is a NASDAQ listed company, with USD$146 million market capitalisation as of September 2018.

When you visit the website, Travelzoo will ask you which country you are in. The deals on the Australian site appear less frequently than on other sites, but they are still good. I immediately saw a 15-day cruise, and because I know that Neil has a bit of a thing for cruises, I showed it to him. He has spent years researching cruises and uses several travel comparison sites. Travelzoo came up cheaper by around $10 a night.

That said, we did not find this website was as good for airfares as some other travel websites.

Many of the travel packages at Cudo, Scoopon, Groupon and Travelzoo are similar—sometimes they are even the same. I liked the variety of Travelzoo options, especially as they were not just geared to the Aussie traveller. When I visited the Chinese language site, for instance, I got a different range of options tailored to a Chinese-speaking tourist.

DAILY DEALS

Blink and they're gone! If you see something you like on a daily deal website, you had better act quickly, and the owners of these online sites and apps are hoping that you will do just that. They are mainly about selling products rather than services, and generally they offer pretty good value.

E-commerce is changing. It is becoming more international, it is becoming more varied and it is becoming more mainstream. It is now acceptable, even normal and common, for people to buy clothes online, whereas five years ago, most people would not have dared. I even bought a wedding dress online (it didn't fit, but that's another story).

These sites can be useful for birthday and Christmas presents. Of course, it is cheapest if you have the 'conversation' about not buying presents at all, but in some social situations presents are hard to avoid. (Like the first Christmas with Neil's family—celebrated while he was in hospital after his heart attack.)

The big problem with these sites is that browsing them can become seriously addictive. Because they rely on impulse buying, they cater to profiling that 'must have do-dad that you never needed before but absolutely can't do without now'. Postage can also be a killer. Look for deals that give free postage over a certain amount. Also, consider doing a group buy with friends to reduce postage or even get it free.

CATCH OF THE DAY

I became addicted to Catch of the Day last Christmas. I found it was an easy way to do my online Christmas shopping, especially as I could take advantage of late November Black Friday online shopping specials. I liked the fact that the parcels were delivered to me; while I pretend to be anti-consumer, I just love the thrill of receiving packages and opening them up.

While I enjoyed the Catch of the Day experience, I did find some of the same products at the same or even cheaper prices at other discount stores, such as Chemist Warehouse. That said, as I have young children and am time poor, I loved the convenience of being able to shop at home and order online.

When Catch of the Day was a new concept, it offered one, or maybe two, items and they were available only for 24 hours. The range has now expanded, and items are often available for longer. However, the line-up changes every day, and you need to snap up most items quickly to lock in the special price. I have been caught out a few times when I have pondered for longer than I should over items in my cart, only to find that the prices changed or the items were no longer available.

AMAZON (INCLUDING AMAZON AUSTRALIA)

No discussion about e-commerce is complete without mentioning Amazon. Amazon began life as an online portal for selling books, but it is now a global e-commerce platform and technology provider. It has reshaped e-commerce in the United States and in many other countries.

When it entered Australia in late 2017, many analysts and merchants expected Amazon to disrupt the market by offering cheaper online deals and faster delivery. This did not happen — at least not yet. Many of the deals offered by Amazon Australia are not as cheap as its competitors, although its big advantage is that it is easy to use because it warehouses the items together and ships them together. If you order several items through eBay, for instance, they are shipped through different vendors and so they arrive at different times and you have to pay shipping costs from each vendor.

CLICK FRENZY

This Australian site only offers items for sale once a year, on 15 November. Although the big sale only happens once a year, the site does offer a few other events throughout the year. As the name suggests, it is all about frenzy and encouraging shoppers to snap up a bargain quickly.

The items are only available for 24 hours. Click Frenzy works with a range of retailers, many of whom are already discount sellers, to offer special discounts. The response is so overwhelming that the site often crashes. I'm not a huge consumer and try to shop for things I need rather than random cheap products, so this is not the site for me. But I suspect I will still end up stopping by for a peak each year.

MYDEAL.COM.AU

MyDeal.com.au is an Australian e-commerce platform that, according to its website, has shipped over two million parcels since it was founded in 2011. It offers a range of lifestyle products, at competitive prices. It is hard not to find a good deal on this website.

LIGHTINTHEBOX.COM

Light in the Box is a Chinese-based site that offers goods direct to the public. With the rise in global e-commerce, sites like these will become more common. It makes sense: since many items are imported through a middleman from overseas anyway, often China, why not buy direct?

Online reviews for Chinese-based sites vary. I find that people who have had bad outcomes tend to go online and rant more than people who are genuinely happy with their purchase. Your recourse for compensation may be limited if the product doesn't suit or you don't get what you want—Australian consumer protections can be difficult to access (my experience is that they are next to impossible, especially if the company does not have headquarters in Australia). My advice is to pay on your credit card via PayPal. That way you effectively have 90 days insurance on PayPal if something goes wrong, and you might have other avenues of compensation with your credit card.

I purchased a wedding dress from Light in the Box for $200. I loved the colour—champagne—but the style wasn't right when it arrived. It was unflattering, and Neil told me I looked like a pumpkin. But it delivered exactly what I asked for. I was nervous when I placed the order because the online reviews were mixed. However, I felt reassured when I found out a good friend had bought her wedding dress on the site.

ALIEXPRESS

AliExpress is a retail site for consumers, linked to the giant Chinese e-commerce site, Alibaba. It works especially well for odd stuff you might buy from China anyway. It is more like eBay than a daily special, although it does have regular specials, such as Chinese Singles Day on 11 November each year.

Based on my own experience, the products on AliExpress are often imperfect. However, it is much cheaper and in many cases faster than comparable products on eBay. While much has been written about market disruption by Amazon Australia, I feel that AliExpress is poised to take a much larger market share in the future.

WISH

If you are regularly on Facebook, chances are that you have come across Wish. Wish ads pop up with all sorts of suggestions, many of which are hilarious and a testament to consumer society gone mad. It appears to customise ads depending on consumer preference. For some reason, Wish keeps sending me pictures of $19 Princess Bride wedding dresses, a cat suit with a slit up the back (the model usefully poses to demonstrate how this can be used in an adult context — enough said), male underwear designed to medically assist dangly bits (with diagrams!), a $2 plastic contraption that allows women to wee like a man (useful for camping, perhaps?), men's suits from $7, and cocktail dresses. Neil has been receiving ads for men's underwear that supposedly allows for better airflow. Intrigued, we searched for men's underwear on the Wish app. I learnt more than I ever want to know about kinky men's underwear — if this is what you are in the market for, Wish has it for you.

I have not purchased through Wish (no, not even the cat suit). I have contemplated buying something because it is so cheap, but have been a bit hesitant as the reviews suggest that quality is often poor. My sister said she bought a few things through Wish and found them to be poor quality. If I was planning to buy a $19 wedding dress, I would probably use it for dressing up rather than a big do at the Hyatt. You never know, though — you might be lucky. How closely does anyone really look at a wedding dress? You only wear it once, and it's all a bit of show in any case.

One annoying feature of Wish is that you might see something you like flash up on Facebook, but you cannot click to go directly to the product and buy it. This is because Wish is solely an app-based platform, so you need to download the app, remember what the item was, and then search for it. Once you have downloaded the app (as I have done), you get pinged regularly with good deals. When you are in the app there are plenty of prompts to remind you of good deals, so there is little danger of missing out.

CASHREWARDS AND SHOPBACK

But wait, there's more!

Just when you finally found yourself a fantastic deal through Cudo, Groupon, eBay, Amazon, Chemist Warehouse, Finder or Scoopon, you could also get cash rewards from using CASHREWARDS or ShopBack.

CASHREWARDS is an Australian-based online platform. According to the *Australian Financial Review*, it had 365,000 local members and annual revenue of over $12 million as of April 2018. Retailers pay to be included on the platform. When you click through to retailers via the CASHREWARDS platform, you get a cashback reward. This can vary—mostly you'll get 2 or 3 per cent back, but sometimes it can be up to 12 per cent for specials.

ShopBack, which began operating in Australia in May 2018, is a similar concept. The Singapore-based company is already active in Singapore, Malaysia, Indonesia, the Philippines, Thailand and Taiwan, and processes 1000 orders every hour, according to an article in the *Australian Financial Review*.

ShopBack claims to be able to offer consumers up to 30 per cent cashback on purchases with over 500 online brands, including The Iconic, Booking.com, asos, Menulog, AliExpress and Catch of the Day. Co-founder Josephine Chow told the *Australian Financial Review* that they plan to take on major brand partners in the lifestyle space 'that impact the average Aussie's daily habits'.

It takes an additional step to order through CASHREWARDS or ShopBack, and it is easy to forget. Last year Neil booked an airline ticket to Europe through STA for a special price of only $1300. After he booked, I realised he could have earned $6 cash back. Not worth the bother? If you take an 'every dollar counts' approach, $6 can buy a lot of food at ALDI. One way to avoid forgetting is to install a plug-in. That way, you will receive an alert whenever you are on a site that has cashback offers.

Both CASHREWARDS and ShopBack offer 'refer a friend' incentives.

As at the time of writing, CASHREWARDS offers $10 each for you and a friend that you refer, and ShopBack offers $5.

THE PROMO CODE ADVANTAGE

You have done your research online for the best deals. You have found the items that you want and they are all in your cart, and you are about to checkout. As you fill out the payment details, there is one final detail you can include that will save you money: the promo code.

A promotion (promo) code is provided to customers as a short-term incentive. It might be something like 'TAKE5' that gives $5 off to customers. Or it could provide a percentage off a purchase as part of a special promotion. Sometimes if you leave items in your cart and hesitate for a day or so, you will receive an email from the company reminding you to purchase the items, and giving you a promo code that you can use for a discount. However, sometimes if you leave items in your cart for too long, the special deal will no longer be available (or sometimes the cart gets cleared out). Sometimes you might find a promo code on Facebook or other social media.

Even if you haven't been sent a promo code, you can still use one. You don't have to be in a special club or clique to be allowed to use a promo code; the fields on the computer that ask you for a promo code do not discriminate as your order is being finalised.

Every time I am about to make a purchase online, I stop when I see the words 'promo code' and do a quick search. For instance, if I search 'Kogan promo code', I'm presented with an array of options.

There are many websites that trawl the internet looking for the latest promo codes. Some do it to lure you in so that you can search for other deals on the site. You may find that many of them have expired, or that they are not relevant. But you don't know unless you try.

There is now an online extension program that searches relevant promo codes for you automatically. Honey is free to join. Once you've installed it, it pops up automatically when you are about to pay for products online. It then scans for possible promo codes. Honey also encourages users to submit promo codes that they know work.

I like the concept of Honey, but Neil did a trial for me that did not fill me with confidence. He found that Honey was slow to work as it took time to trawl through several options. In the end there were no promo codes suitable to the Australian-based sites he used. He believes that it might be more applicable to online sites in the United States.

This is one to watch. Although Honey might not work well yet, it may get better. There might also be other products in this space that tap into promo-code sharing with greater success.

FRUGALISTA CHALLENGE

Your challenge is to find and use a coupon or voucher to get a discount. Maybe you might go out for a special meal with a partner or friend using a great Groupon deal, or go early and use First Table. Or perhaps you can apply for CASHREWARDS so you can earn some cashback on products that you would otherwise purchase, or try an e-commerce platform that you haven't used before. Whatever you choose to do, record how much you save. How much could you save in a month on purchases that are genuine needs — $10? $20? $50? $100?

CHAPTER 9

ATTRACTING WHAT YOU WANT

How to get stuff for free

THE FREE ECONOMY

Download for free. Buy one, get one free. Sign up now and get a set of steak knives for free. Watch this free video that will change your life. 'Free' is often used as a marketing gimmick designed to suck you in. However, 'free' is often the frugalista's best friend. Things can be genuinely free, and even ethical.

Around a third of the clothes in my cupboard were free. Much of the food in my pantry was as well. Some of my furniture was free, and many of my books too. When I was planning my wedding, I got lots of things for free. How is this possible?

Before I spill the beans on how I get things for free, let me first delve into the relationship that many people have with 'free'. When we receive something for free, we often think it is substandard, or somehow dodgy, as if we are desperate and needy and need to steal things. Receiving charity is, we often think, something for the poor.

We all love the allure of a good bargain. A friend of a friend was once decluttering and wanted to get rid of a sofa from her house. She listed it online for free, and there were no takers. Eventually, she put it out on the nature strip with a price tag—and it was gone in an instant.

The value of something is often a notion in your head. Of course, if you went out and bought the materials or ingredients and made something from scratch, you would know exactly how much it cost you. However, if you already have something in your home, the value is relative. For example, perhaps you paid thousands of dollars to buy an Italian dining suite. But if you then decided to move overseas to study in Europe for 12 months, you might be so desperate to get rid of it that you would give it away for free to avoid having to pay for storage.

We are seeing this trend play out in many Western societies, such as in Australia and the United States, with ageing parents who have stored up antique furniture, crystal, doilies, lace tablecloths and bric a brac that they planned to leave as heirlooms to their children. The only problem is that their kids don't want it—they often live in apartments, or they have enough of their own stuff. These items would have been expensive to buy in their hey-day, and many would have been cherished wedding presents. They played an integral part in household entertaining and witnessed celebrations of key events.

However, now they are too big and bulky to fit into modern homes, and stylistically they are too dark and heavy. Instead, they are being shunned for flat-pack furniture that is often less durable (and in some cases made under doubtful labour conditions). Some people are complaining that they can't even give away the old stuff; even if they can sell it, prices are much lower than in the past. As an article in property magazine *Domain* noted, children expecting their parents' estates to be worthy of *Antiques Roadshow* are often disappointed.

As for me, I rejoice in free things that I receive as part of the abundance of the universe. I accept them with gratitude, acknowledging the spirit of love in which they were given. I try to remember to say 'thank you', and to practise genuine gratitude.

The cycle of receiving also involves giving. I believe in 'paying it forward' by giving freely and generously of my own things. I believe that people and community are more important than 'stuff', and I try to practise that by putting more value on people than on stuff.

I also believe there is a karma in giving—and receiving. When you give things with love, I find it often returns to you multiplied. It doesn't always return from the person who received your gift, but often it returns in unexpected ways. I tend, for example, to be lucky on a consistent basis with raffle tickets and other awards. But then, that reflects the fact that I often purchase modest amounts of tickets to support causes I believe in.

Not everyone is so lucky. I remember trying to sell raffle tickets for the Rotary club I was a member of in Taipei. 'I never win anything,' said a man brusquely when I offered him the chance to purchase one. I could have told him that if you never buy a ticket, you are never going to win a prize, but I bit my tongue. Meanwhile, I bought a few tickets and ended up winning a night in a luxury hotel. As I said, I am often lucky.

There are strong environmental, social and ethical aspects to the free movement. Many of the formal organisations that I have detailed in this chapter were established to avoid things being dumped into landfill. Many items can be recycled in innovative and interesting ways. Or something that your family has outgrown (e.g. baby clothes, cots and prams) might be perfect for someone embarking on a new beginning or transition.

This is my philosophy of 'free'; it is not about taking to fill a selfish need. Nor is it about stealing. It is being part of a community and social cycle that puts a value to items that would otherwise be wasted, or that assists community members through sharing.

So, where do you get things for free?

JUST ASK YOUR COMMUNITY

Imagine you are baking a cake and you realise you have run out of eggs. Do you a) bundle your young kids, who have runny noses and are cranky, into the car and drive to the shops and battle a supermarket queue? Or do you b) knock on your neighbour's door and ask her for two eggs?

Most of us would sooner be independent and go to the shops rather than rely on others. However, for years I lived in a quiet cul-de-sac in suburban Canberra surrounded by lovely neighbours. We nicknamed them our million-dollar neighbours because they were such amazing people and it felt like we had won the lottery by living next door to them. On more than one occasion, I knocked on Libby's door and asked to borrow a cup of sugar or an egg or whatever I needed. She was always happy to oblige. From time to time I would drop off home-baked goodies, and I hope they also thought I was a good neighbour. They weren't my only close neighbours; my good friend Sue would regularly drop off homegrown roses or vegies and stop by for a cup of tea. She even started to teach me how to sew.

If you don't have close neighbours, what is stopping you from making some? Not only could you gain the occasional cup of flour, but it could save you in more significant ways. In 2003, devastating bushfires raged through Canberra suburbs, razing 500 homes to the ground. Many people were still on summer holidays at the coast.

Who would you call if your street had to be evacuated and people were on holidays or at work? Would you think about the old lady across the street or the stay-at-home mum, on her own with kids and no car while her husband was at work?

Realising how little people knew about their neighbours was a real issue that people living in many suburban Canberra streets faced at the time. It led to the emergence of strong community groups in some areas. Even 16 years on, many areas in Canberra have regular street get-togethers. Christmas events are big, as are annual trick-or-treat functions for kids.

This isn't the only time that communities have rallied together after an emergency. Neil, who is active in the Rural Fire Service (and who recently received an award for ten years' service), told me about his experience of the 2016 Carwoola bushfires. The Rural Fire Service communications team put together a 'telephone tree', which is a list of people in the community and their telephone numbers, and asked people to phone others to check on their wellbeing. This was especially important given many properties were some distance apart.

It is often said that it takes a village to raise a child. Or children. Or to save your sanity, especially in an age where increasing numbers of people are suffering from depression or anxiety. Community linkages, once seen as old-fashioned or quaint, are more important than ever. It is therefore unsurprising to me that much of the 'free' movement focuses not just on stuff, but on the interconnectedness between people.

Perhaps you don't happen to live in a middle-class suburban Canberra cul-de-sac. (I no longer do, either, having moved to an inner-city apartment.) However, being part of a community is vital. For some people, that community might be online via social media networks.

Have you ever thought about asking for help from your friends on Facebook?

Maybe you need to borrow a trailer, or need help with moving house, a cake pan for baking a wedding cake, a lift somewhere, a particular book, or homegrown lemons. You never know unless you ask, and you might find that your friends or family have just what you are looking for.

Perhaps it seems daunting to ask directly. Another approach could be to casually mention in conversation that you are looking to buy something or planning to do something. If you attract frugalista friends, as I do, you may find someone who volunteers to give you what you need. For instance, you might mention that you are planning to set up a herb garden on your balcony and that you are looking for cuttings and pots. Your friend might then volunteer some herb cuttings, plants or seedlings that she has and maybe even some old pots.

LET PEOPLE KNOW THAT YOU LIKE FREE THINGS

On more than one occasion, people have given me food from their cupboards. It is usually something they plan to throw out, either because they are moving or because it is almost out of date. Recently I even had a lovely lady drop off several boxes of foodstuffs that were just past the 'best before' date (which is only intended as a guide). It was all perfectly fine and I received it with thanks.

On several occasions, people have said things to me like, 'Serina, I'm giving this to you because I know you won't mind. I hate to throw this stuff out, but I don't know many people who would like to have it. Most people like to buy things new these days, and I feel embarrassed to give them a half-opened packet.'

If you have open conversations with friends and family about how you like to help the planet by reducing waste, or if you freely offer things of your own that you love but no longer need, you will be surprised to find that people start offering you things.

My policy is to always accept with gratitude—unless I know it's something I really won't use. I then find a way to 'pay it forward', such as by making a cake for other people to share, or by passing on clothing to friends who I know it would fit better.

THE 'BUY NOTHING PROJECT'

I admit to having a bit of a Facebook addiction. I have signed up for more groups than I have time to participate in actively. Of all the groups that I belong to, my favourite is my local Buy Nothing Project.

Are you a member? If not, I strongly suggest you go online NOW and search for your local group. My experience with this group has been life changing (in a good way), and my wish for you is that you have a similarly fabulous experience. If you are already a member, I would love to hear about your favourite Buy Nothing Project experience.

Buy Nothing Project is a hyper-local organisation that is all about reducing waste. However, it is much, much more than an organisation that reduces the amount that goes into landfill. Instead, the Australian-founded global movement is aimed at community building.

The Buy Nothing Project is a Facebook-based platform, which operates via Facebook groups. You must live in the local area of the group that you wish to join. I was in an active group in my outer-Canberra home and had to say goodbye to that group and join a new one when I moved to the inner city. I was sad to go as I had made some strong friendships. I hosted a swap meet during my last week in that house and, although I was trying to declutter, I came away with a whole bag of things that I have used over and over.

Thankfully, I was welcomed into my new group, and I am now meeting new people. My new group has already become so large that it has split once, and is about to split again in a process that is known as 'sprouting'. The idea is that if a group gets too big (in this case over 1000 members), then it loses its community feel. So, the group sprouts a new group, and the process goes on.

How do you get things for free, you might ask? Members of a group post items that they want to gift, and then people in the group put up their hands for anything that they want to receive. No money changes hands (it is not allowed), nor are you allowed to ask for anything in exchange. You do not have to prove that you are destitute, or worthy, or that you would put the item to better use than someone else. You do not have to be the first person to put up your hand. You can also ask to loan items, offer services or ask for help.

For instance, I was recently decluttering and wanted to give away a Kathmandu hoodie that I used to wear when first in Canberra. It was perfectly fine, but I used to wear it when I was with my ex-husband, and it was time to move on. I also wanted to create space in my linen cupboard, so I offered some quality bed linen. These were both picked up by a lady who needed them, and I dare say the hoodie will fit her much better than it fit me.

A weekend earlier, I put up my hand for some baking supplies. I scored a silicone macaron baking sheet, several cookie cutters and some adorable fondant cutters. I spent the next day creating plum blossoms out of fondant and dreaming about whether I could bake and ice my wedding cake. I am far from being a professional cake decorator, but with the right tools I ended up creating an impressive 1950s-style three-tier cake adorned with shimmering pink sugar roses and plum blossoms. I shared some of my flowers as a gratitude post on the group, and another member told me how she made her wedding cake—and offered her cake pans.

Over the years I have received furniture, ski clothes, children's clothes, jewellery, clothing, kitchen utensils, household appliances, jars and food through the Buy Nothing Project. I estimate that I receive around $1000 in value every year from the group, and it saves me a fortune by allowing me to declutter things that I no longer want.

However, it has been the friendships, connections and information about the growing contra-consumerism movement that has meant more to me than anything else. I am proud to be part of the Buy Nothing Project movement, and I am sure it will continue to enhance my life.

OTHER FACEBOOK GROUPS

In Canberra, there are a whole host of Facebook groups that support the free economy. Examples of such groups are Canberra Freebies, Canberra

Free Things Only, Free Stuff Canberra and Surrounding Areas, and Canberra Buy, Swap and Sell. Since Canberra is much smaller than many other capital cities—or even regional towns—I am assuming that there will be other similar groups in other areas.

If you put the word 'free' into a Facebook search engine, you will find many options. This is especially good for people on low incomes who are genuinely in need. However, it is a resource that anyone and everyone can access.

You can also find free things in Facebook Marketplace, the platform established by Facebook to rival eBay, and other online buying and selling sites. On a recent search, I found sofas, filing cabinets, single beds, packing boxes, a wig, coffee tables, children's outdoor playground equipment and a dining table with eight chairs.

Often a condition of 'free' items is that you must collect them yourself. However, these days people can be so keen to get rid of unwanted stuff (often quickly) that they will gladly deliver to you.

FREECYCLE

Freecycle is the grandaddy of the free movement. At the time of writing, the Freecycle Network was on its way to 10 million members globally (to be precise—9,333,146 members in 5323 groups), according to its website. Founded in Tucson, Arizona, in 2003, it was one of the earliest platforms to encourage gifting. It was certainly the first recycling and gifting platform I heard of, and I thought it was revolutionary when it first came on the scene in Australia. One of my close frugal friends did much of the landscaping of her front garden with the help of items obtained from Freecycle. I have done well out of it myself through the years.

For a long time, Freecycle operated as a Yahoo! Group, and it never migrated to Facebook (unlike other groups). Thus, it was a little more unwieldy to use than the Buy Nothing Project. Its platform now appears to be mainly web-based, so you no longer need to sign up for a Yahoo! email account.

I used to love Freecycle and once became glued to it during a stay-at-home holiday. I watched it all day, waiting for free things to appear. However, these days I no longer use it and wondered if it still existed.

What changed? I moved away from using my Yahoo! email, for one thing. For another, the culture in my group lost its 'loving feeling'—or maybe it never had it. I found that people tended to gift to the first person who said they would take something, and it became a bit of a race to get in first. As items could be offered anywhere throughout Canberra (including Queanbeyan and surrounding areas), the collection could often be difficult—especially with little people in tow.

However, more than that, I think the problem was with (as termed by someone else, not me) 'ungrateful people'. There was a culture of no-shows—people who wanted items but would not collect them. Some people wouldn't look you in the eye or talk to you when they collected items. I am unsure if this was from a sense of shame at having obtained 'free' things, or because they were shy. It certainly wasn't true of everyone, but being a larger group, you did not build close relationships.

I find that the focus on local communities in the Buy Nothing Project encourages a completely different dynamic. Sometimes it takes longer to gift an item, and there is not the same range, but I love the feeling of being connected to my community.

GIVIT

If you work in a charitable organisation dedicated to poverty reduction, then GIVIT is something you may wish to investigate. Similarly, if you want to feel sure that your decluttered items go to a worthy cause, and that you are giving a charity what they need rather than burdening them with excess, GIVIT could be a great platform for you to use.

According to GIVIT's website, Juliette Wright established GIVIT in 2008 after she tried to donate second-hand baby clothes, only to find that the charities needed other items. She recognised that there was no portal through which charities could reach out to the public to ask for what they needed, so she developed a platform that allowed for matching between donors and recipients. The platform rose to prominence after it was used as the Queensland State Government's official website for matching donors and recipients during the catastrophic 2011 Queensland floods.

The website has a list, able to be sorted by postcode, with short (and tear-jerking) descriptions about who needs the items and why. Children in refugee families who need school uniforms and basic clothing. Basic kitchenware, cutlery and utensils for a new migrant family who want to cook and eat at home. A bike and helmet for a young refugee boy who wants to play with other kids and feel included (imagine not having the money to allow your child to cycle with other kids in the street). Ski jackets, not for snow sports but for homeless men sleeping rough during bleak Canberra winters.

These are just some of the many stories of people who are in need. It's hard not to feel moved, and perhaps even confronted, when reading this list. It certainly made me appreciate how comparatively prosperous I am. While this chapter is about getting things for free, I hope this information helps someone you know who is struggling; if you are also looking to declutter, GIVIT is worth checking out.

THE BARTER ECONOMY

I recently had a chat with a friend at work about his Japanese-inspired vegetable garden. He has a Japanese wife, spent many years working in Japan and is fluent in Japanese. He grows Japanese-style gourds, and Japanese and other Asian greens that are not commonly found in shops.

'Maybe I could swap items with other people,' he mused.

Perhaps the universe heard us, because a few days later a 'Grow Free' stand appeared in a corner of the work cafe. People from work began bringing in herbs, vegetables, lemons, limes, chillies and tomatoes. The idea is that they gift them for other people to take as they like. It's lovely to discover what items are gifted, and to be able to share in this way.

In addition, there are several Facebook groups dedicated to the barter economy — including BarterEconomy Canberra. The idea is that you offer items that are surplus to your needs (e.g. lemons from your tree) in exchange for something someone else has in excess (e.g. eggs from their chooks). You might struggle to be entirely self-sufficient using the barter economy, but it can work well when you have excess produce in your garden and want to swap it for something in return.

An extension of the barter economy is the 100kilos.org project. Formed by Canberran Elizabeth Goodfellow in 2014, it facilitates a harvest swap. It aims to encourage people to grow more fruit and vegetables, with the website also providing tips on how to grow more food at home.

I participated in a few harvest swaps in 2015, which were conveniently held at my local fruit and vegetable market. The way it works is that you bring along some produce that you have grown at home (in my case it was some cherry tomatoes, rosemary branches and zucchini). You deposit your items, and then you choose freely from the produce that other people have contributed. I found it was an effective way to diversify my diet. No matter how optimistic I used to feel at the prospect of harvesting my first zucchini, by the end of the season I was sick of it.

GUMTREE

Gumtree is my go-to site for cheap second-hand items. It's a treasure trove for unusual items, listing thousands of items in Australia and the UK.

However, Gumtree is not just for buying and selling—it can also be used to list items that are free. Just search your location and 'free', and you will see a list of many items.

Why would anyone give away things for free when they could sell them? For several reasons, a principal one being time. A friend at work moved in with his girlfriend and needed to declutter in a hurry. Consequently, he sold things cheaply and often gave them away. I once gave away a second-hand double bed mattress; I wanted it gone, and in my single-mother life, going out and hiring a trailer and taking it to the dump was too complicated. It was picked up within a day by a man who rented out a room in his house.

Our lives change. You move in with someone, get married, have kids, your kids grow up, they move out, you move overseas for work, you get divorced, you downsize in retirement—there are many ways in which your life can change. Sometimes these changes happen quickly, and that is when that comfortable, yet no longer new, sofa needs to be ditched in a hurry.

THE LOCAL TIP

Your local rubbish tip might seem like an odd place to go to find free things, but you could be surprised. These days, most councils and local governments have active waste management programs that include encouraging recycling and reusing.

Here in Canberra, there is a shed attached to the tip called The Green Shed. It is a seriously cool place for frugalistas and environmental warriors. You can get all sorts of things there that are very cheap—it's like a giant op shop except it also has broken objects just waiting for someone to fix them. They also give out clothes for free. They receive so many clothes that they would rather give them away than see them being thrown straight into landfill.

The first time I saw this free clothes area I was doubtful. However, a quick rummage through showed that there were some surprisingly quality items in there. I especially liked a thick, hand-knitted woollen cardigan that someone's nana probably spent hours making. No-one need know that something was free if it looks good on you. Even if it isn't perfect, perhaps it could be remodelled or reused somehow.

RANDOM THINGS BY THE SIDE OF THE ROAD

In some areas, you might be lucky enough to have council-organised kerbside pickups where you can put out old furniture and other household items, and the council will collect and dispose of them for you. They no longer do this in Canberra. However, they do offer it in Queanbeyan for pensioners.

Although we no longer have formal collection programs, a strange culture has emerged in inner-Canberra suburbs; people often leave furniture, books or bric a brac by the side of the road for people who might want them to collect. Sometimes these items will have signs on them — more often they do not. It rarely rains in Canberra, so the items don't tend to get soggy being left out in the elements. People in my local Buy Nothing Project group often take photos of items and share them so that others can collect them.

The system is not organised, and I keep waiting for government officials to issue an edict forbidding the practice. However, I assess that it is not only harmless but a positive cultural development. It says much for the environmental consciousness of the people in the area in which I live and speaks to their generosity. There is an unstructured free-spiritedness to it that I like. I'm sure many items end up in university student share houses.

STREET LIBRARIES

Do you have excess books at home and have thought about lending them to someone? Street libraries do just that. They are ever so cute — they look similar to a mailbox, but they are in fact a free lending library that people put out the front of their house. Some are even architecturally inventive. The idea is that people take a book they want, and replace it with another book. It's a way for neighbourhoods to share with each other. It makes sense: how many times do you read that Harry Potter book you have on your bookshelf? Wouldn't you rather it went to a primary school kid who will read it with the same wide-eyed wonder that you once did?

The movement started in the United States, where they are often called Little Free Libraries. The website says there are over 75,000 such registered libraries in over 85 countries. They exist in Australia, too. Nic Lowe founded the Street Library movement for Australians in Sydney in November 2015. You can go online and find the nearest Street Library or register a new library at streetlibrary.org.au.

I don't have a Street Library in my apartment block. However, my church has one. I found a fabulous book about recipes for people with food intolerances, which I gave to a friend at work who found it useful. There is always someone who would welcome the random books that are sitting unloved on your bookshelf.

THE LOCAL LIBRARY

When I first moved to Canberra, I worked with a man who was very conservative, even by Canberra standards. He was a lovely guy with high moral standards. 'What are you doing this weekend?' I asked him one Friday afternoon. 'Well, I'm going to the library,' he answered.

At that stage in my pre-kids 20-something life, I had other weekend plans that did not involve the library. However, when I did get around to visiting the library, I discovered that it was very cool. Not only can you borrow books at my local library, but also magazines, CDs, DVDs and audiobooks. The library even has energy savings kits that enable you to measure energy usage. You can stop by and use the internet and printers—I no longer have a printer at home, so I do this whenever I need to print a document. There is a range of free talks and activities, especially some fun sing-along sessions for young children. Best of all, there is an amazing online range of e-books with a wide selection. My local library also gives me access to a range of online magazines and even resources for learning foreign languages.

Every time I go to the library, I estimate I come away with hundreds of dollars' worth of books or other items. For free—as long as I remember to return the books on time so that I don't get fined. And as long as I don't lose any (yes, this has happened in our household). If you are on a budget, it is worth checking out what options your local library has. A night at home with a free book or DVD could be a rewarding and relaxing evening.

COMPETITIONS

A blogging friend of mine always seems to win competitions. His secret? When the contest requires an answer in 25 words or less, he writes a poem. He has a clever sense of humour, and his short poems always make people smile. How could you not want to give a prize?

Meanwhile, my Auntie Glenda often wins prizes on radio contests. She has a favourite radio station, and when the announcer says, 'ring in and tell us for your chance to win', or 'first on the phone'—she is on the phone. She wins a lot.

As for me, I win at least one or two things a year. My favourite place to win prizes is a free publication, *The Canberra Weekly*, which has regular giveaways. A few months ago I won a night out to watch a

Johnny Cash and Roy Orbison tribute performance. The tickets were over $60 each, yet we were able to walk in for free.

I nearly always take the time to go online and enter contests when there is an opportunity to do so. Someone needs to win, and that someone could well be me.

The exception to this is when a contest requires you to buy large numbers of a product to enter. If I have a use for the item, and if it is cheap, then maybe I will buy it so that I can enter. However, in most situations, I find that the money spent on a chance is not worth it.

BLOG IT OR VOLUNTEER IT

In my food blogging life, I get given freebies. This includes invitations to restaurant launches, 'meet the chef' opportunities, cocktails, tourism events and all sorts of other events.

A word of warning: there is no such thing as a free lunch in the food blogging or social media context. While others might be relaxing and enjoying their meal, I am busy putting out Instagram photos and writing notes about the dishes. It takes several hours to produce a blog post and to share it. For me, it is something I enjoy doing, and I love supporting local businesses, so it is a privilege to be invited to such events. However, if I counted all the hours involved, it certainly would not be worth quitting my job to do it. Of course, if I become a blogging mega-star, the situation might be different, but for now it's a fun hobby.

The point is that if you have a passion for something (in my case, food), then there could be a way that you could get products or experiences for free in exchange for promoting them on social media or other platforms.

You could also get something for free by volunteering. For instance, my friend Trish volunteered at the Folk Festival in Canberra this year. In exchange, she got a free pass, which was worth hundreds of dollars.

Did she volunteer so that she could get into the event for free? No. Trish is a generous, warm-hearted person who volunteered because there was a need. Local performance events often need volunteers, and if you have the time and interest, you could end up being part of some amazing events for free.

These are some of the ways that you can get things for 'free'. There are many different pathways, and this is just the tip of the iceberg. The main idea I want to convey is that abundance is everywhere when you take the time to look for it. Further, it is okay to accept with gratitude the abundance that the universe provides. Something free is not automatically substandard, nor is it wrong (unless, of course, you stole it). When you open your mind to the free economy, you might be surprised by what is out there.

FRUGALISTA CHALLENGE

Attract at least one free thing this week. Maybe it will be something from the Buy Nothing Project, or maybe a gift from a friend. Perhaps before going out to buy something, you could put out a request on Facebook to see if anyone you know has what you're after. Accept with gratitude, then pay it forward by giving something back to someone else.

CHAPTER 10

CAN'T BUY ME LOVE

Money and relationships

TALKING ABOUT MONEY

Money is one of the biggest sources of friction in relationships, especially in affluent countries such as Australia. Yes, money seems to create more tensions when you have it than when you don't. I think this is because the more money you have, the more expectations there are that it should be spent pursuing a certain lifestyle. When you have children, there is also tension about what to spend on them, and also the decision of whether a parent should stay at home and, if so, for how long.

According to a survey on Australian attitudes towards money and relationships that was conducted by Greater Australia Bank, one in 20 Australians feel uncomfortable talking about finances with their partner. The results do not surprise me (I thought the rate might be even higher), but I still find it shocking. The fact that you can be in a relationship with someone and share so much, have children together and even buy a house, yet not feel comfortable talking about money is scary. This is especially true when you consider that the same report identified that 82 per cent of respondents said money caused tension in their relationships, and nearly one in five people (19 per cent) experienced a relationship breakdown due to money. Such financial problems can easily lead to a phenomenon known as sexually transmitted debt.

So many aspects of relationships are dictated by marketers, who tell us we need to pay money to buy happiness. Whether it is online dating sites, expensive dates, long-stemmed roses, diamond engagement rings, big weddings or romantic holidays, the marketing world tells us that money *does* buy love, and you need to spend, spend, spend if you want to be loved. Is it any wonder that sitting down and doing a budget together to work out how much this all costs can be scary? Deep down many of us are scared that we might not be loved if we don't have enough money.

Why is this happening? My experience tells me that it has a lot to do with different values about life, which affect how you spend money. It also has a lot to do with the marketing mishmash we have been fed that tells us money is essential for romance.

If you see a financial planner or get advice as a young person on how to invest and manage your career, someone will likely produce a graph for you. These are financial plans that chart off into the distance, based on assumptions that you will continue to invest in logical and consistent ways. Based on assumptions of earning X or saving Y, of starting work after finishing university and retiring at age 65, getting married at age 28 and having 2.2 children, you can expect that you will end up with $XYZ. This is a nice plan. Except that life does not go to plan.

You might get married early, then divorce. You might never marry and instead be in a de facto relationship. You might marry the love of your life but be unable to have children (or choose to adopt stray dogs or cats instead). You might marry several times. Your partner might die before you (or you might lose more than one significant partner to death). You might decide that you want to conceive and bear children without a partner. You might be perfectly happy as a single person, or you might choose to live a polyamorous life. Or maybe you are lonely and seeking your soulmate online.

The point is that our lives rarely go to plan. And when we are in relationships (or if we are trying to get into relationships), we tend to act in irrational ways when it comes to our finances. Discussions about money and investing tend to assume logical, rational behaviour. However, when we are in relationships, especially relationships where our money values are not in sync, we tend to act in illogical ways. Maybe we avoid talking about money, or assume the other party is providing for us, or blame the other party for spending too much (even as we go shopping ourselves), or let the other person make the decisions so as not to rock the boat. Perhaps we spend too much trying to make the other person happy, or we don't make savings or investment decisions that we think we should, because we worry our partner might not agree. We buy that caravan they wanted (or we think they wanted) and spend up big at Christmas to try to be generous towards the in-laws in the hope that they might accept us. We go guarantor for a loved partner or an adult child in a business because we want to support them and for them to succeed, never thinking that our future could suffer if things go bad.

Of course, you can also be in a happy relationship where you share similar money values. Many successful people talk about the vital supporting role their frugal and supportive spouse has played in their success. Many uber-wealthy, such as Warren Buffett and Mark Zuckerberg, got married in their own backyard or that of a family member. When a couple are working together with common goals — including saving and investment — they can achieve some amazing things.

I want to share with you openly some of my own experiences about relationships and money. Then I want to delve into some areas where many would not dare to tread: the cost of courtship and romance (including online dating), heading down the aisle towards commitment, and how you handle joint expenses.

MY STORY — RELATIONSHIPS AND MONEY

Let's start at the beginning.

I was in a relationship with my ex-husband for 17 years. We met when we were both at university. He had just migrated to Australia from Taiwan. He had a law degree from Taiwan that wasn't recognised in Australia, and had enrolled in a law degree at the University of Queensland. I was over halfway through my law degree at the same university and doing an Honours degree in Chinese studies, and had been offered a scholarship to study in Taiwan. A mutual friend, who I studied law with, introduced me to my ex.

We were language partners at first and then over time, grew to become more. We started dating ten days before I left to study in Taiwan for a year. He visited me when I was in Taiwan, and later we were posted (with my work) to Taiwan together.

Neither of us had much in the way of savings when we first met; both of us were students for several years before I got a job as a public servant in Canberra in 2000. I moved first, and he followed me. We saved hard and bought a house in 2001, just as prices were skyrocketing (it was good timing). I remember at the time that our $229,000 four-bedroom, two-bathroom house seemed exorbitantly dear—we subsidised it by hosting homestay students, which we did for six years.

We lived together for six years before we got married. Our wedding was a cocktail reception at my mum's place on the Gold Coast—a Queensland wedding was much easier for family, including my ageing nana. My mum made my dress and the bridesmaids' outfits. Our honeymoon was a trip back to Taiwan (with my mother-in-law!), made possible in part because Taiwanese friends and family gave red envelopes (*hong bao*) filled with money, as is their tradition.

In one sense we had similar money values, but in another sense, it was a major source of tension. We both committed to a life of saving money to buy investment properties—at the time of separation we had ten properties in total. A workmate once joked, a tad disparagingly, that we were 'very Chinese' in how we lived: we stayed at home, rarely ate out and saved, saved, saved to buy properties.

The tension came because I felt that our negative gearing was too extreme. And I wanted to have fun.

After eight years of intense budgeting and saving, we had our first son, who was born two months prematurely. Anyone who has given birth to a sick child knows how stressful that is, and knows about the medical costs that seem to go on and on. I took nearly seven months of maternity leave. Perhaps I might have taken off more time, but I was worried about paying all our mortgages so when an opportunity to go on posting to Taiwan came up, I grabbed it.

Living overseas on posting was extremely busy, made even busier by caring for a young baby when I came home from work—and then having another baby while on posting. My ex-husband did not adjust well to his role as a trailing spouse, and I felt he struggled with his loss of identity.

But it was also a glamorous and exciting time—banquets, dinners, cocktail parties and receptions. They were all after-hours events that took me away from my family, but they were also fun. After so many years of staying home on Saturday nights watching television or playing Scrabble, I loved the high life. I loved exploring Taiwan and finding out about the quirky mix of ancient temples and the modern cafe culture metropolis. I also started writing when the kids went to bed on a blog called Taiwanxifu—Taiwanese daughter-in-law—about being the wife of a Taiwanese man.

What went wrong? Well, many things and it culminated (back in Australia after a difficult time overseas) in me taking out an interim domestic violence order in August 2014. The Magistrates Court granted me a second order in August 2015. It was a difficult, dark time that was made more difficult by money worries. We were over-geared with our properties, the rental market had dropped (one property had been vacant for six months), and I was paying childcare for two boys—Canberra has the highest childcare rates in Australia and some of the highest in the world. I was also paying legal fees of around $500 per hour.

Looking back, we had a huge clash of values regarding money. He wanted to invest for the next generation—to buy lots of properties and leave a legacy for our children. Meanwhile, as the main income earner, I was the one who bore the burden of making the mortgage repayments. I felt constantly stressed, and my dreams of being able to do things like travel to Positano in Italy, caravan around Australia to visit wineries, or write a book seemed to become increasingly unlikely.

Financial abuse is nearly always a factor in domestic and family violence. In some cases, it is overt—for example, a woman who is given a tiny allowance by her husband to live off or has been discouraged from being in the workplace. In other cases, it is more subtle. In my case, I felt frustrated that I did not feel as if I had an equal say in how our money was being spent. I also felt that I was the one who made more financial sacrifices. In short: I felt like I was a chequebook rather than an equal partner and wife.

It probably cost me around a quarter of a million dollars to get out of my marriage, and there are still ongoing costs. If you ever wonder why women don't 'just leave', know that money is a big part of it. I am thankful that I have a stable public service job, also that we had solid investments that (mostly) performed okay when sold. I do think that much more needs to be done to understand and support working women who leave bad relationships.

Coming out of this, I had to live an extremely frugal lifestyle for a while. The first six months were the hardest. I remember that first Christmas. I didn't have much money but splurged on cheap plane tickets to take my boys to Melbourne to be with family. I re-wrapped some birthday presents so that they would have gifts to open. I had just paid some large utility bills and, while I was managing, I felt that things were fragile financially. I pulled out of a heavy-handed court process my lawyer had insisted on as I didn't have the money to pay her. Perhaps I would have been in a better situation now if I had seen it through, but it would have broken me financially and emotionally.

Still, I felt blessed, especially compared with others in my situation. I volunteered at my church's Christmas hamper appeal that year and it was so humbling to see that there were women in very similar situations to me who were so much worse off. At least I had a job, I could pay my utilities, and I had some presents for my kids (plus I could afford to fly to Melbourne, albeit with tickets bought on sale).

During this time, I was still writing and blogging, but more about food and lifestyle issues. I felt like my frugal living (that was more of a necessity than a choice at the time) was something to be a bit ashamed of. But then I realised how important my financial resilience was: because I could live on the smell of an oily rag, I knew I had the resilience to create a new life for my kids and me. I decided to turn something that would otherwise be negative into a positive, thus the genesis of my blog, which led to this book.

Suddenly single with two young boys, and not feeling flash about myself, I didn't expect that my chances of getting into a new relationship would be all that high. But unexpectedly, seven months later I became involved with a blogger I met in the Canberra social media scene. Sadly, it didn't work out. I felt devastated at the time: the whole relationship was intensively passionate and had come out of the blue, and then just kind of burned out.

Afterwards, I felt broken and lonely. Added to this were some difficult property negotiations with my ex-husband and some work stress. I dealt with it by going onto online dating websites and chatting.

At first, it felt like a guilty secret. It had been years since I had been on the dating scene and, to be honest, even the first time around I didn't do the 'scene'. Some of it was sleazy and much of it was desperate. As a single mother with young kids, it was hard to get out and socialise. I was always clear that I was committed to behaving with integrity, but clearly not everyone reads. I learnt to have thick skin and to stand by my values. It seemed like everyone I met assumed that promiscuity was permissible, and indeed, the way things were.

Through this, I met a guy on Tinder (yes, Tinder), who later became known on my blog as Mr Red Sports Car, on account of his M Series BMW. In his first message to me, he stressed that he was a man of integrity with strong family values. From the first time I met him in person, we clicked (or so I thought). He was a sales executive at a multinational high-tech company (one of the largest in the world), successful and confident. I loved our banter about innovation and I felt that he encouraged me to aim higher.

He was not frugal.

After our second date, he mentioned that he was house hunting. Intrigued, since I like property, I asked him to send me details. The townhouse was listed for $1 million.

He did not seem at all fazed by the price tag. That night, as I was driving him to our third date in my (then) 16-year-old Toyota RAV4 (with my kids' peanut butter crusts littered over the back seat), I had to ask. 'So, what's your financial situation? Are you totally loaded and thinking of buying that place with cash?'

'Well, I will need a mortgage, but I don't know how much I will need to borrow until the family house sells,' he answered. 'I have a good job that pays well.'

His job, I soon learnt, paid him nearly four times what I earnt — but much of it was commission based, so it varied from year to year. He also came from a wealthy family, where everyone else drove Mercedes, and he tried to live up to their standards.

He certainly lived the good life — he wore tailor-made suits, invested in artwork, bought more expensive personal grooming products than most women, and enjoyed dining at expensive restaurants. I was getting a steady stream of invites to restaurants and cultural events in my blogging and professional roles, and he loved the VIP treatment we received. I enjoyed having a corporate executive to accompany me and, if I am honest, I felt flattered that such a successful man was interested in little old me. I felt bedazzled in the same way I imagine Cinderella felt with the attention she received at the ball.

He tried hard to convince me that we had similar values, but I always felt a bit conflicted with how different we were. He liked going out to eat, or if we stayed at home, watching rugby union on one of his two big-screen televisions while drinking expensive shiraz (he had a cellar of over 800 bottles—no $5 bargain-bin specials or cask wine for him!) and eating steak that cost more than my weekly food budget. I, on the other hand, am not really into competitive sport, owned a small television that I rarely switched on, was formerly a vegetarian and only drank alcohol when I had guests (and even then, only with dinner).

I became concerned about his money decisions. He was struggling to finalise the property settlement with his divorce (he had separated a year before I met him), yet he seemed to keep spending and spending. Rather than sell the family home, he ended up buying out his ex, moving in and financing it through a $1 million interest-only mortgage. His wine collection kept growing, and he thought nothing of buying things on his Amex card.

My mother, always an insightful woman, told me that it was fine to date him, fine to go out and have nice dinners and good sex (yes, she said that!), but under no circumstances was I to marry him. 'Darling, you will end up having to support him,' she said. 'You've worked too hard to get to where you are.'

And there were hints that this would have been the case. 'Would you still love me even with all of my debt?' he implored one night as I drove him home from a prosecco and vintage muscat tasting event I had been invited to, and which he had partaken of liberally. On another occasion, he took me to dinner, again got drunk, and joked that I would support him in his old age in the manner to which he was accustomed.

I was not impressed and told him so. The money jokes stopped. I was keen (after having been in a controlling relationship) to retain my independence, especially on financial issues. I did not want anyone, particularly his kids, thinking I was using him for money—especially as they themselves appeared to be doing just that. I remained focused on my frugal goals, and in fact paid off my house while we were still together. I wore op shop dresses on dates.

But still, being around a hyper-consumer corrupted me. I reciprocated his restaurant meals by taking him out. I bought Dior perfume online rather than the chemist bargain-bin knock-off specials I used to wear. I took out a credit card for the first time in years, 'just in case' I needed it when we were out together. I felt embarrassed by my suburban home, and (after paying it off) moved to an inner-city apartment where I hoped he would visit more often. He wanted to travel, so we went on an overseas trip to Taiwan, where we stayed in four-star hotels rather than Airbnb. He would have preferred the Hyatt, but it was out of my budget, and I insisted on paying half.

I felt a bit like a second-hand rose—the woman who didn't earn so much and who was frugal and frumpy. He didn't introduce me to many people, and when he did he seemed a bit distant, so I just assumed it was because I wasn't beautiful or successful enough. Looking back, it said more about him than me, but at the time I thought I wasn't good enough.

Perhaps you can guess where this is headed, but the fallout took me by surprise.

We spent Christmas 2016 with my mum and stepdad on the Gold Coast—he invited himself to Christmas lunch because otherwise he would have been alone. We then headed to Taiwan together, where

I played tour guide and interpreter for a week. We saw in New Year's Eve with friends, watching fireworks on the rooftop of their house. I was in love, and Taiwanese friends commented that they had not seen me so happy in years. But when we got back, he began to get busy and was increasingly distant.

Four months later, I broke up with him because he was clearly not into me. We remained friends and spoke regularly—he had promised me early on that we would always be friends no matter what. Three months later, I discovered via Instagram that he was involved with a younger Taiwanese woman: he met her while we were on holidays together in Taiwan and he began his involvement with her while he was still dating me. They loved the high life—five-star hotels in Asia, chardonnay by the pool, shiraz in the bedroom, French Champagne in private dining rooms. While I will never know the true nature of their relationship, he represented it on social media as a young Asian woman with her sugar daddy. He even used descriptions like #asiancutie and #asianpersuasian to describe her.

I felt sick to my stomach. For months I couldn't sleep properly. But I also felt thankful that I wasn't stuck married to him, picking up the tab on his rendezvous with another woman; that could easily have ended up being the case.

There was a silver lining to all of this.

I felt gutted during the break-up. I felt like I had lost a close friend and couldn't understand what I had done wrong. But I also felt empowered. I made a choice not to accept sub-standard behaviour ever again. I made a conscious effort to love myself and, above all else, to embrace my values. This included frugal living, integrity, love and honesty. I committed to living a 'gold standard' life and to modelling ethical behaviour in everything that I did. In today's social media age that can sometimes be hard, and I'm still often faced with choices where I am not exactly sure what the best course of action should be.

Let me say, the bikini butt pictures of his better-looking and younger love interest did not make me think that my new ethical, frugal lifestyle was especially exciting. I felt like a boring, middle-aged pumpkin. But I held fast to my values.

Through it, I found myself. And I met Neil.

Two weeks after I split up with Mr Red Sports Car, I had a tense phone call with him. He was on holidays in Thailand—later I would discover he was with his new Taiwanese girlfriend, doing cooking classes together and drinking gin and tonics on the hotel balcony. I didn't know that then, but I do remember thinking, 'If you don't appreciate me, I'm going to meet someone decent who does.' I hopped online and signed up to RSVP as soon as I got off the phone, drying my eyes and taking some glamour selfies. Two weeks later I did, in fact, meet the love of my life.

Not that it was love at first sight. I thought Neil was a decent, honest country boy—a bit scruffy, not intellectual, heartbroken, but with a heart of gold. No fancy European sports car here, but a sturdy ute that he drove to and from his country property. I told a friend that I thought Neil needed someone who could join his local CWA and bake scones and go on caravan trips with him and sing together by the fire. (It turns out his dad loves my pumpkin scones, we have Friday karaoke nights, and I love his caravan, but that's another story.) I thought I wanted to live the social high life revolving around a cool inner-city existence, and I didn't think we were right for each other. Yes, I was a bit of a snob.

Meanwhile, Neil thought I looked like an Oompa Loompa (the short people who work in Willy Wonka's Chocolate Factory). He thought I was interesting, passionate even, but not especially attractive.

He asked me out for a second date. I said no. He asked to be friends. I said yes. He said he was relieved because he was going on another date that week in any case. He asked my opinion about how he could make a good impression on the other lady.

Somehow, oddly, we became increasingly close friends. We chatted online constantly and would ring each other after a date to report on how it went. We shared nearly everything about how we felt with each other. I gave him good dating advice, which he used back on me (without me realising it). We became flirty, and he certainly tried it on; he was persistent. After two and a half months he made a move on me while I was cooking a lemon and cream pasta for dinner (he had invited himself over, not for the first time).

By then he had become my best friend. It was scary to become romantically involved with my bestie, and I worried I might lose him from my life. However, it grew into a beautiful relationship built on shared values. Four and a half months later we were engaged. We joke that Neil's heart attack, nine days after our engagement, was related to the engagement, but it had likely been building for some time and showed us how life is fleeting and cannot be taken for granted.

Neil is frugal like me. I worried at first that I was coercing him into a frugal lifestyle, but one of his adult daughters assures me that he was always frugal. We shop at ALDI and Costco, he picks up things for me from our local Buy Nothing Project, and he even found the matching navy pure wool jackets that he and his best man wore at our wedding at op shops — for a grand total of $19.50 for the two jackets.

We share the same strong tea bag when making each other a cup of tea in the morning. We happily go on dates where we use Entertainment Book specials, or we stay at home and have karaoke Fridays with a home-cooked meal of fridge leftovers and a bottle of homemade ginger beer. We talk openly about money, including how we manage our superannuation and our day-to-day budget. We bought investment properties and started share investing within months of being in a relationship together. He is handy and is good at doing minor repair work in my apartment and our investment properties. He fixed my bike when I kept cycling over sharp weeds and pumps up my tyres for me.

Our values come from different money conversations we grew up with. My parents separated when I was eight. My mother was a successful businesswoman. She loves property, and at home, we talked about buying and selling property all the time. We looked like the wealthy jet set on the outside, but we shopped at bargain supermarkets and did food prep for the week together on Saturdays. I did not grow up expecting a knight in shining armour to take care of me, and consequently, I do not look for that in my relationships. Nor did I plan to take off a lot of time to be with my children when they were young. To be honest, at the time I didn't even consider it because I had never experienced that traditional role of a mum as a homemaker. Instead, I have a powerful mentor who made me believe that I could achieve anything I wanted to as a woman.

Meanwhile, my dad worked as a Commonwealth public servant for 52 years. He retired with a solid defined benefit superannuation fund, which means he gets a pension for life. He is big on community service, and it was largely through his encouragement that I joined the Commonwealth public service myself in 2000. He wants me to stay in my secure public service job; I feel honoured to be able to serve my country, but I keep having radical, innovative ideas and feel the calling to be an entrepreneur. In my public service roles, I sometimes feel like I haven't achieved anything tangible, and that I am not helping people to make the best of their lives.

Neil's parents had four children at a very young age. They didn't have a lot of money, but they made do. His dad was serving in the Navy during the Vietnam War when he and his sisters were young, so his mum did much of the work of raising them. They didn't have a lot of 'stuff' as they couldn't afford a lot, but they did have a lot of love. His parents retired in a modest but comfortable fashion, with no mortgage, no debt, and defined benefit superannuation and a veteran's pension that allows them to go on a cruise at least once a year. Neil also started a family when he was young. His conversation about money is more conservative than mine, but we are similar in that we both value family and financial security over flashy toys and 'stuff'.

For me, I love that cup of tea with the shared tea bag every morning and the joy of building a simple but loving life together. It is the small things to me that make a relationship—the shared laughs, meals together, ability to negotiate differences so they don't turn into conflict, and crucially, showing an interest in the things that are important to the other person. Research by the Gottman Institute on what makes a successful relationship reveals how showing interest in the other party ('Turn Towards Instead of Away') is crucial to a happy and long-lasting relationship. A happy relationship has nothing at all to do with how many carats are in a diamond ring, and the positive goodwill engendered by treating your other half well will last long after the long-stemmed red roses have faded and died. And best of all, it costs very little.

THE WORLD OF COURTSHIP

'We met through mutual friends,' or 'We met at high school or university,' used to be the way couples met. However, according to an article on dating statistics published on the dating website Zoosk, since 2017, more people have met their soulmate online than through other means.

I remember my mum being concerned that I was online. Certainly, some apps such as Tinder have a bad reputation for encouraging hook-ups. (I was on Tinder at the same time as a Christian minister I knew—it has a broad audience.) But it's not all that bad. Chatting with people online allows you to vet them a bit and to establish a rapport before meeting in person. You can even check them out on LinkedIn or other social media before agreeing to meet face to face. When done well, it can be safer and classier than getting drunk at a bar and letting someone chat you up using corny pick-up lines.

According to that same Zoosk article, 19 per cent of brides said they met their husband online. This is significant because the figure was only 5 per cent of American couples in a 2015 Pew Research poll, so the use of online portals to meet and marry seems to be growing. Interestingly, research also suggests that despite the negative stereotyping about online dating being linked to uninhibited sexual behaviour, couples who meet online tend to get married sooner and the marriages are less likely to end within the first year. I guess you wouldn't be online unless you were after a relationship, and you are more likely to talk about the fact that you actually *want* a relationship than, say, flirting with a colleague in the kitchenette at work and hoping he/she isn't gay, already married or going to report you for sexual harassment.

The issue is the cost.

Loneliness is big business. A 2005 article in the *Sydney Morning Herald* reported that RSVP, the platform on which I met Neil, was purchased by Fairfax media for $38.92 million. That was before online dating had taken off in the way it has today. And as for Tinder, in late 2017 it was reported in a CNBC article to have over 2.5 million paid subscribers (some analysts assess that only 5 per cent of Tinder's users are paid subscribers). Match, the parent company of Tinder (which runs other online dating sites as well, such as OKCupid), has a market capitalisation of USD$11.63 billion, according to Yahoo! Finance, which also assessed that the global market for online dating services (currently about 500 million) would rise to 672 million by 2019. Some online dating sites such as Tinder have a free interface but charge for additional premium services.

I like how Tinder operates. I like the speed at which it works and the way the interface is designed. What I dislike is the way the Tinder culture has evolved to mainstream the assumption that people on it are 'only' looking for hook-ups and kinky sex. The good thing is that you can unmatch someone, and that's what I often did.

It has now been over a year and a half since Neil and I first chatted online on RSVP. I was quite brazen and paid for the first 'stamp': Neil told me that this was the first time a woman had ever been that bold with him. Overall, RSVP is an expensive online application, and it annoyed me that it hadn't evolved to embrace many of the innovations that Tinder and other apps had. Messaging other people through the platform is expensive and clunky.

Several single friends or friends newly in relationships have told me that they like Bumble. Bumble gives power to women as they must approach a man rather than the other way around (it also caters to same-sex relationships).

My cousin, Sara, is an avid Bumble user. She said that she gets more genuine responses using Bumble than other dating apps she has tried. So far it hasn't cost her anything to use the app. She used it when on holidays as a way to socialise and meet people, but in the past she clearly articulated that she wanted a relationship. She has had two relationships with men she met on Bumble. It didn't cost her anything, other than her time, to meet them via Bumble. Most of Bumble's services are free, but you can pay to access premium features through Bumble Boost. Bumble has over 12 million registered users and claims it has led to more than 5000 engagements and weddings.

Online dating platforms provide a service and they will cost you money to use them. The big players are making big money. Do your research before purchasing, just as you would any other service. Sites like productreview.com.au can help, as can research from trusted consumer organisations. Also be aware of the importance of ensuring your privacy and avoiding scams. Never send money overseas to someone you have met online, for instance.

WHO WANTS TO DATE A MILLIONAIRE?

Would you date someone who earnt less than you? This is an interesting question for me, as in my previous marriage I earnt more than my husband and that did cause friction. According to the results of the Greater Australian Bank survey mentioned above, one in eight Australians would not date someone who earnt less than them. But the report notes that money isn't everything: three-quarters of respondents would prefer a partner who was poor but attractive, versus rich but unattractive. I guess having a sugar daddy isn't everything.

I earnt nearly double what my first husband did. When we met at university I had a part-time job and so had more money to spend. Money was not a factor in our romantic attraction. However, I will admit that, after my separation, I turned down dates with guys who did not seem to be well off financially. Now that I am in a good financial situation and have two children to raise, I was a bit cautious about having to support someone else. Does that make me shallow? To my credit, I also turned down dates with some high net worth individuals because we didn't click.

Money always features on dates, even if it isn't as overt as someone bringing along their payslips for you to pore over. When you are on a first date with someone (or even before you get to that), you want to project an image of being financially successful—or having the ability to be so. Who wants to date a loser with no drive or ambition?

On the subject of dates, who pays? This was something I struggled with in my post-divorce dating adventures. I did a rough poll online because I was interested to see what other people do on dates. Of the 53 votes received, 89 per cent said that they would let the man pay and 11 per cent said that the woman would pay. Twenty people (mostly women) said that it would be best to split the bill. Reasons for doing so included personal safety (not creating expectations or being owed anything), or because it was important for the sake of equality. One of my female friends said that she always insisted on paying on a date.

When I was dating, I generally let the man pay (shock horror). I would also generally let him choose the venue. I sometimes offered to pay, and on one occasion my date said he would welcome splitting the bill and I had an awkward moment where I couldn't find my purse in my Tardis handbag (plus we had both gotten a bit tipsy on riesling to counter the spicy food we were eating). So embarrassing.

I consider it a bit like a sales pitch. If someone were trying to sell me their services, I would generally expect they would take me out to coffee or a simple meal to discuss it. I would be under no obligation. That said, I would not accept an expensive meal from someone — especially if I wasn't sure if I liked them or not. It would then feel to me like I was using them.

MARRIAGE

So, you have decided to tie the knot. Now what?

TO RING OR NOT TO RING?

Most women I know believe that diamonds are a girl's best friend, a diamond is forever, and you need a decent carat rock to prove that your man loves you. Ideally, one that cost two months of his salary. After all, you are worth it — right?

Of course, it must be big and special because everyone will want to check it out. But engagements do not always, inevitably, involve diamonds. The phrase 'A Diamond is Forever', coined by a copywriter at the ad agency N. W. Ayer, was part of a successful campaign by De Beers to convince men to buy diamond engagement rings for their intended. De Beers appointed the ad agency in 1938 because the price of diamonds was falling globally due to oversupply.

I believe a woman should think seriously about the cost of a diamond ring before she places it on her finger (note: she might not have a choice if her fiancé thinks she expects one). A diamond *is* forever, and not just because it is a symbol of love. Once you put one on your finger, its resale value drops in much the same way that a new car loses its value when you drive it out of the showroom. I'm speaking as a woman who has two diamond rings. My engagement ring was valued at AUD$4000 in 2001 when purchased new. I considered selling it last year and was told it could fetch between AUD$1000 and AUD$1500. If I was lucky.

Just browse Gumtree to see sorry tales of men and women desperately trying to sell their once-special rocks for anything they can get. As I experienced, the trade in second-hand diamond rings is not especially lucrative. ABC Radio Darwin reported that one enterprising fisherman in the Northern Territory decided to do a swap, offering an 'expensive engagement ring' in exchange for a boat.

Then there is the risk of losing your beloved diamond. A few months ago, my good friend Erna had her engagement and wedding rings stolen from her hotel room. She had travel insurance, but the company would only give her less than a quarter of their retail price.

Of course, if you like diamonds, love jewellery, and desperately want a ring, by all means get a diamond ring. However, make sure that the diamond has a Kimberley Process certification to ensure that it is not a conflict diamond. You don't want what should be a symbol of love to be a blood diamond that facilitated conflict.

If you want lots of bling, consider a synthetically made diamond — it has the exact same properties as a naturally produced diamond. Or even a semi-precious stone. I love my prasiolite (aka green amethyst) ring, which matches the colour of Neil's eyes. It cost a fraction of a diamond that size. Also investigate online options, which can be much cheaper than bricks and mortar stores. My ring was purchased directly from the jeweller via online arts and craft site Etsy, and was custom made to size.

DO I NEED A PRENUP?

I remember once reading a Facebook thread about prenups. Many (mostly women) on the thread were opposed to signing the document because of the belief that if you love someone, you should trust them. Tell that to the thousands of people who get divorced each year, including those where there has been a significant breach of trust.

In Australia, Binding Financial Agreements (BFAs, colloquially known as 'pre-nuptial agreements') have been in existence since 2000. They have been around in the United States and other jurisdictions for much longer.

Ahead of our wedding, Neil and I had been contemplating whether to enter into a BFA. So, I had a chat with Ann Northcote, of legal firm Farrar Gesini Dunn. According to Ann, a BFA is not so useful for a young couple starting out together — unless one party already has a lot of assets or expects to receive an inheritance. They are more useful for second relationships where one or both parties have assets.

A BFA is not a financial plan. It cannot set out how both parties will manage their money during a relationship, nor does it set out lifestyle issues such as who will put out the wheelie bin each week. And it doesn't spell out how assets will be treated after death (this is the work of estate planning — in other words, you need a will).

The BFA is a 'dead document', which only comes into play if the couple separate. It can be useful in providing more certainty about the situation both parties were in when they started. It removes the jurisdiction of the Family Court about property issues, so it needs to be drawn up with great care. For example, if a man left his wife while she wasn't working because of kids and the BFA set out that he would retain the house he had before they were married, the woman could be in a vulnerable position.

If you have assets that you want to protect in the event of divorce or separation, a BFA could be an effective way to do it. It is important that it is well drafted and that you think through the implications of the document. It is not going to protect you from every financial calamity that may befall a marriage (e.g. gambling addiction), but it can make things clearer.

THE WEDDING

With the cost of the average wedding being $51,245 (as reported by 9Honey), and the recent wedding of Meghan Markle and Prince Harry costing around $60 million, what is a modern bride to do?

My advice: say no to tradition and do it your own way.

Neil and I set our wedding budget at $5000. In the end, our 200-guest wedding cost us less than $3000. We saved money through online wedding invitations, sourced clothing at op shops, had friends take photos and asked people to bring a plate rather than give an expensive gift. We were married in my church, surrounded by my community and then had a party in the war memorial hall in Neil's rural township.

We are happy with each other and didn't need a wedding to prove it. However, we both wanted to formalise our commitment together, and as both of us have strong family values, we wanted to bring together our extended families. We also wanted to have a big party after what has been a rocky patch for both of us.

I stressed and stressed over my first wedding, wanting to get everything just right. My sister, Spring, told me that no-one would care about the details, and all they wanted to see was two people in love. I was insulted at the time, but having since been to some weddings where love was not necessarily in the air, I see her wisdom.

If you have fun, your guests will have fun. If you are stressed, your guests will be stressed.

I have been to big, lavish weddings and my experience is that they are not always better. If the speeches are too long and if the atmosphere is not right, no-one will have fun, no matter how beautiful the bride is and how much the couple (or their family) paid for the event.

Research also shows that a more expensive wedding does not make for a happier marriage. In fact, according to a 2014 *New York Post* article, brides who spend USD$20,000 or more on their wedding are three-and-a-half times more likely to end up divorced than those who spend less. And couples who have 200-plus guests at their wedding are 92 per cent more likely to get divorced. (I am hoping Neil and I are in the lucky eight per cent!)

MANAGING JOINT FINANCES

How do you manage money with your partner? Do you have joint finances? Or do you manage things separately?

With my ex-husband, I advocated for a joint account as I wanted visibility over where the money was going. Neil and I had separate accounts for the first ten months of our relationship. Then, when it became clear that we were working towards joint financial goals and had similar financial values, we set up a joint bank account. Managing this requires a high degree of communication between us.

I find that the joint versus single account decision is highly individual. The question of how we manage money in a relationship is rarely talked about — you might, for instance, tell your girlfriends that your husband snores, but rarely would you divulge your banking details. Nor do you often discuss with others how joint purchases are made.

One of the key areas for disagreements in a relationship is around how money is spent. Maybe one side is more frugal, and one side is more of a spender. Or there is the *perception* that the other party spends more. Without getting into the tricky area of the gender gap, let's say that a source of disagreement is how you spend money.

Last year I read a horror blog post. A woman said that she paid for everything, and her husband paid her back. He put the expenses into a spreadsheet but was often slow to do so. She calculated that he was thousands of dollars behind in paying her back over the course of the previous year. She didn't see this as a problem per se; they were in the honeymoon phase of their marriage and still happy and in love. But having just gone through a divorce property settlement, this story filled me with horror.

A good friend told me about a handy app called Splitwise. It's a simple accounting system used for tracking expenses. It can be used for a couple in a relationship, or for housemates. Each party downloads the Splitwise app and enters in whatever they spend money on. You can choose to 'split' equally with the other party, or one party might pay the full amount. It helpfully points out how much you owe the other party, or how much they owe you. It is not the only financial accounting app on the market, but it is a good one for couples or flatmates.

First you must have an agreement about what goes into Splitwise as a joint expense for it to work.

I insisted Neil and I start using Splitwise around four months into our relationship. The pivotal moment was sitting down to a Chinese dinner one night en route to visit friends on the coast. I thought we should try to avoid McDonald's for a change, thus a fancy restaurant. At least, 'country town Chinese restaurant' fancy.

'You can get this,' he said after we ordered.

I didn't mind, but I had just paid for beer and wine to give as presents for our friends. And a gift voucher for his father's birthday that week.

Later I mentioned that to him.

'I forgot about the alcohol and the voucher. I meant to pay you back,' he said. 'Oh, and I also paid for the petrol to the coast and grocery shopping during the week.'

It made me realise that it's easy to remember what I pay for, and easy to overlook what Neil pays for. We have similar frugal values and similar incomes. I have more expenses related to my boys, and he has more expenses related to his car, motorbike and caravan (and he came to the relationship with a bit of credit card debt), but mostly it balances out. It helps to be able to track what we are each spending, so we know where things stand. It also promotes visibility and helps answer the question: where has all the money gone?

THE MONEY TALK

Nothing seems to strike more dread between a couple than the prospect of sitting down and talking about money together. Some people will do anything to avoid it.

Friend and money blogger Kirsti McQueen from iheartsimpleliving. com wrote a guest blog post for me recently, in which she suggested that in any relationship one party is better at managing finances. This is not a bad thing so long as the other party knows where to find key financial information. The issue, though, is to make sure that both parties are on the same page about where you want to head financially.

I think it's important to talk about money from the very beginning of a relationship. It's a little easier for me now because since I am an out and proud money writer, people I know are aware that I like talking about money. Here are my suggestions for having a money talk with your partner:

1. **Schedule a date semi-regularly, at least at the end of the year and the end of the financial year, for a dedicated money chat.** These dates are triggers for reviewing your net wealth progress because they enable you to set your financial goals for the year ahead and then to review them. Ideally, aim to meet quarterly, but life does tend to sneak by quickly.

2. **Make your money chat a fun event.** Organise to go out (with laptop) or do it at home over a nice meal and a glass of wine. Talking money can be empowering and enriching.

3. **Avoid blaming the other party.** It is so easy to criticise the other party for spending too much, not earning enough, or picking shares that didn't go well. You cannot fix what is in the past, but you can go forward with a loving attitude.

4. **Have conversations based on abundance.** There is power in what we say and the words we choose. Rather than saying things like 'inflation is going up, and things are always getting more expensive', or 'I'll never get promoted', as a couple make an effort to acknowledge your blessings and abundance. A conversation that celebrates getting things on sale or how fabulous it is that your financial situation is getting better can be very empowering.

5. **Talk about money regularly and share information.** I'm a bit obsessed with talking about money. Neil and I send each other news links about shares we are interested in or have already invested in, property news and all sorts of things. We discuss whether to buy more shares, whether to increase superannuation contributions and how much to allocate towards travel. We talk about money all the time. It is so lovely to have someone that I can talk to about these things, and it has given our relationship an added depth and dimension. It is a shared interest that we are developing.

6. **Keep an open mind about your significant other's ideas.** Maybe you think that the prospect of buying an investment property is too scary, or the entrepreneurial shark tank idea your spouse has is crazy. But you never know: it might just be the best thing ever. I regularly say

'when I'm a billionaire' as if it is already happening, and I don't care if Neil thinks I am nuts. He never laughs at me or dismisses my 'out of the box' ideas, which is part of the reason why I dared to write this book. Support your other half by listening rather than dismissing, saying 'yes, and' rather than 'no, but' as you tease out ideas. When you are in a supportive relationship, you can have the courage to do amazing things.

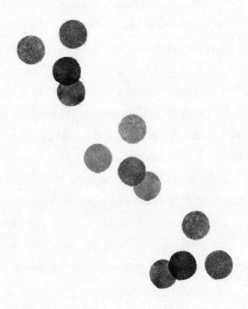

INTERVIEW WITH KIRSTI MCQUEEN FROM IHEARTSIMPLELIVING.COM

What are the important money lessons you have learnt through your relationships?

The most important money lesson that I have learnt is to have the early confidence to talk about your relationship with money, as both an individual and a couple. In my first marriage, my husband saw himself as the financial decision maker because he earned more money while I cared for children. I hated not being a financial decision maker with a passion.

In my new relationship, I observed my husband's money habits and I realised that he was generally frugal and sensible—in 2008 he told me his main goal was to pay off his mortgage (then around $350K) and that piqued my interest. I liked the sound of that. And then I observed he owned a vintage Porsche—and I had trouble reconciling this in my mind. How can you claim to have a mortgage goal and own a Porsche? Well—turns out you can. As Paula Pant says, you can afford anything, but you can't afford everything. David prioritised his love of cars and when he spent money on cars, he derived great pleasure. And it was his hobby—he would order parts and replace them himself. Otherwise, every cent went on the mortgage.

The other relationship saver is that we both have allowances. From our salaries, all money goes into a *joint account for expenses, no matter what they are. Fundamentally, David and I do not like to compare the costs of my children versus his. We also believe that we can achieve greater financial goals, like FIRE (Financial Independence, Retire Early) if we work together. So instead, we have generous allowances—$300 a fortnight—to spend on anything we like. I used to spend mine down to the last cent on clothes, haircuts, bags, girls' weekends and make-up, but this year I am saving it all in an index fund to create a passive income allowance stream for the future. So far this year with savings and some eBay sales, I have saved $5000.*

Finally—even though I am the one in our relationship passionate about finance—we discuss everything. If I can see David's eyes glazing over I stop (sometimes!), but I like to make sure he agrees with my decisions around investing and our FIRE goal. It's critical to have shared financial goals so you can come back to those goals when making individual investment and spending decisions.

Having worked as a family lawyer, what are some of the money issues that you have come across?

Primarily, that one person in the relationship takes on the financial management responsibility and the other partner has no clue. It's much easier to give up the responsibility and not have it weighing on your mind.

I think the best way to address this information imbalance is for the financially keen partner to agree on financial goals with their partner and then create a book, locked up in the safe with the wills and powers of attorney, with all of the relevant investment, debt and account details, so that if you get hit by a bus, your partner knows where to find everything.

Secondly, I have seen a lot of women not caring much about super. Even though it has future financial benefit, some women would rather take cash now and not split the husband's superannuation for future benefit. This is an issue where women have taken on primary carer responsibilities during the marriage, and consequently have a lower superannuation balance. There is an increase in women living in dire financial circumstances post-divorce at later stages in life. I think when you are separating from your partner, the most sensible thing to do is to get both family law AND financial advice, so you don't cut short what you could otherwise be entitled to in the future. Of course, you need to balance immediate needs with future ones, but please, get financial advice at the same time. And change your will straight away.

If you don't yet have a partner, it is important to keep in mind the sorts of financial values you want in your ideal mate. This does not necessarily mean trying to snare a millionaire. Growing up, I met lots of rich kids, and few of them had the money sense to be able to hold onto their cash. However, money is more to do with values than dollars and cents. It is vital that you consciously connect with someone who shares the same vision that you do. You can help that process along by writing down the sorts of money qualities you are looking for in your potential life partner, for example, a good work ethic, honesty, living within his/her means, and having good financial literacy.

FRUGALISTA CHALLENGE

Have a money talk with your significant other. Ideally, do this at the beginning of the year and again halfway through the year. Organise for it to be an empowering rather than a fault-finding occasion. Try to use 'yes, and' when talking about money options rather than 'no, but'. Resist the urge to blame your significant other for spending too much.

If you don't have a romantic partner, write down the financial qualities you value in a mate — this is more than hoping for a millionaire who will provide for you, and more about what money values you believe are important.

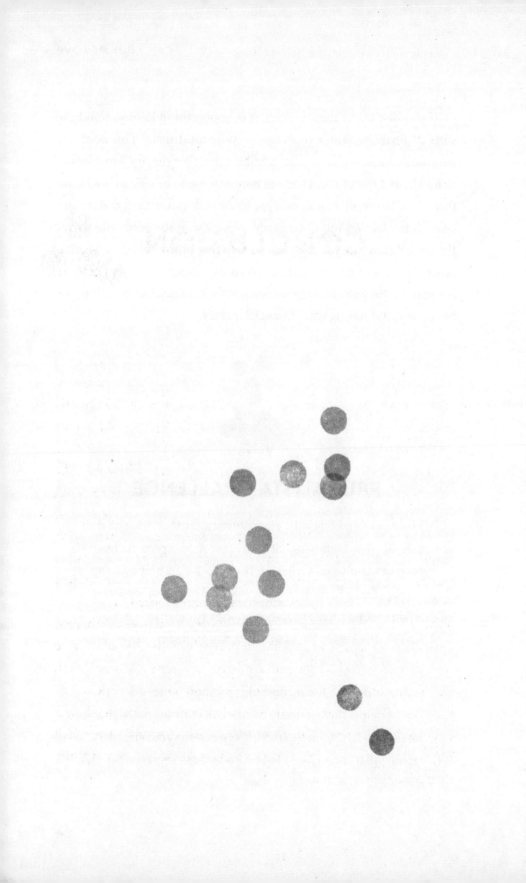

CONCLUSION

This book is about living a joyful frugalista life. It is about saving money. However, it is about much more than that. It is also about valuing and respecting ourselves and others—our friends, family, community and the environment.

It is simplistic to say that all the environmental and social woes of the world are caused by too much 'stuff'. The geopolitical causes are much more complex than that. However, when we approach our own consumption patterns with mindfulness and compassion, taking an approach of thinking about what we need and how best to respect what we have, then it creates change. If many of us do this, then it creates even more change. My wish is that frugalistas become a movement.

When I was looking for a partner, before I met Neil, I thought critically about what I wanted in a man. I decided that I deserved to be with someone who had the gold standard—someone who was honest, decent, full of integrity, involved in his community and respected by friends and family, and who loved and adored me. This all seemed impossible at the time, like an audacious dream. (Actually, when Neil was trying to convince me to date him, he told me that he was better than gold, he was platinum.)

It occurred to me one day that if I was to attract someone with gold standards, then I needed to model that behaviour myself. I always try to behave with integrity, although I must admit that sometimes I struggle with some grey areas—good and bad is rarely black and white. Issues come up from time to time in a work, blogging or even social context that are difficult to deal with. When in doubt, I always go back to the basic premise of insisting on the highest gold standard of integrity and morals. If nothing else, I will always sleep well at night knowing I have strived to make the right choice.

In writing this book, I wanted to articulate how my frugalista lifestyle is an extension of my gold standard. It is about modelling the best possible standards for myself, for the community in which I live, and for the environment. It is about being authentic and true to myself, and striving (in small, everyday ways) to make the world a better place.

I wondered for a while whether any of this matters. In the face of too many tacky social media stars to mention, too many celebrity affairs coming and going, why would a second-hand and money-saving movement matter? But it does matter and it does make a difference. I know that because I understand how living a frugalista lifestyle brings me not only financial resilience but great happiness.

As I type this, I am on a skiing holiday with my dad and Neil. My kids would be here, too, except that they have declared that they don't like skiing (#firstworldproblems). The fire is roaring in the fireplace, and outside a dozen or so wild deer run by. It is starting to snow, and the clouds above the snow-covered mountains are bright pink against the deep blue sky. Later, we will sing some karaoke together, and relive some of today's skiing exploits over a spicy Sichuan hotpot. This isn't a frugal holiday, although we made it possible through a frugal lifestyle and a series of frugal choices—I found a good accommodation deal in the Entertainment Book and Neil even bought second-hand skis on eBay that he waxed and sharpened himself. However, it's more than just a holiday as it's about connecting with people who are important to me, and sharing experiences together.

As to that gold standard, funnily enough Neil said that's what he found most attractive about me—not looking like a gorgeous model or being clever, or having a lot of money. Being a frugalista can be sexy. Just saying.

INDEX

ACKNOWLEDGEMENTS

This book would not have been possible without the encouragement and input of some special people.

I want to thank my dad for being the first one to tell me that my writing was readable, and my mum, who provided a strong role model of a successful, stylish self-made woman. Thank you to my sister, Spring, who always ensures I am fabulously well dressed, and my niece, Kayleigh, for proofreading. I'm grateful to all my Savvy Sistas for their proofreading, input and support. Thank you to Marg for providing literary guidance and inspiration for the book and to Trish for being an amazing frugalista mentor. The ACT Writers Centre provided much-appreciated support, including through its HARDCOPY program; and my literary agent Jacinta di Mase contributed honesty and astuteness. It was a pleasure working with the Murdoch Books team: Kelly Doust, Lou Johnson, Vivien Valk, Julie Mazur Tribe, Justine Harding, John Canty, Lou Playfair and Carol Warwick. And, of course, thank you to my Neil, for believing in me and loving me even when I was a tad stressed while writing this book.

NOTES

NOTES

NOTES

NOTES

NOTES

NOTES

NOTES

NOTES

NOTES